YORK HANDBOOKS

GENERAL EDITOR:
Professor A.N. Jeffares
(*University of Stirling*)

STUDYING SHAKESPEARE

Martin Stephen

BA (LEEDS) PH D (SHEFFIELD)
High Master, Manchester Grammar School

and Philip Franks

BA (OXFORD)
*Professional actor, member of the
Royal Shakespeare Company, 1981–3*

822.3
C697 z1/

LONGMAN
YORK PRESS

D0365867

The illustration of the Globe Playhouse is from *The Globe Restored in Theatre: A Way of Seeing* by C. Walter Hodges, published by Oxford University Press.
© Oxford University Press

YORK PRESS
Immeuble Esseily, Place Riad Solh, Beirut

LONGMAN GROUP LIMITED,
Longman House, Burnt Mill, Harlow,
Essex CM20 2JE, England
Associated companies, branches and representatives
throughout the world

First published 1984
Ninth impression 1996

ISBN 0-582-03572-4

Produced by Longman Singapore Publishers Pte Ltd
Printed in Singapore

Contents

Introduction   *page* 5

Part 1: The background to Shakespeare   7
The life of Shakespeare   7
The historical and social background   11
Shakespeare's theatre   17
The Elizabethan world   27
Reading list   32

Part 2: A general view of Shakespeare's works   35
The plays   35
The sonnets   49
Shakespeare's themes   50

Part 3: Critical introductions to selected plays   56
Hamlet   56
Macbeth   62
Othello   66
King Lear   71
Henry IV Part 1 and *Henry IV Part 2*   76
Twelfth Night   81
As You Like It   86
A Midsummer Night's Dream   90
Much Ado About Nothing   95
Antony and Cleopatra   100
Measure for Measure   105
The Winter's Tale   110
The Tempest   115
Romeo and Juliet, Julius Caesar and
    The Merchant of Venice   118

Part 4: Studying Shakespeare   123
  An alphabetical guide to Shakespeare's style and technique   123
  How to approach a Shakespeare play   130

Part 5: The actor's Shakespeare   132

Part 6: Selected bibliography   143

Index   149

The authors of this Handbook   160

Introduction

The aim of this book is to provide the student studying the works of Shakespeare with a brief, clear, and straightforward source for all the major information he or she is likely to require, and to combine in one volume several of the functions of books on background information, critical surveys, notes, and bibliographies.

Part 1 gives the basic biographical, literary, social, and historical background to Shakespeare's plays. **Part 2** gives a general 'overview' of Shakespeare's work, showing his development as a playwright and the links that exist between his plays. **Part 3** gives critical introductions to some of the most popular and widely-set plays. Part 2 and Part 3 are obviously designed to help the student with individual plays. They are also designed for the student who is studying one or two plays by Shakespeare, and who wishes to 'read round' the plays, and in particular read other plays by Shakespeare. Part 2 and Part 3 point out which plays should be read as background reading, and, without forming the student's opinion, give some critical landmarks in each play, so the student has some idea of the major issues involved, and what to look out for when reading them.

Part 4 gives a guide to Shakespeare's style and technique, and a glossary of technical words and phrases, and some ideas on how to approach a Shakespeare play. **Part 5** discusses the plays from the viewpoint of an actor rather than an examiner or teacher (the area most often overlooked in examination or critical texts), and **Part 6** gives a reading list. Only books of proven worth have been included on this list, and only books which have proved helpful to school, as distinct from University students.

This is a book written by a teacher and an actor who share an immense love and enthusiasm for the work of Shakespeare, and who want to write something to add to the average student's, or average theatregoer's, appreciation of the plays. This is a basic handbook, and it tries in a very minor way to support the plays, not replace them. It should only be bought and used by those who are willing to go and see the plays wherever and whenever they are performed, and those who will read their *Complete Works* of Shakespeare more readily than any critical aids.

Part 1

The background to Shakespeare

The life of Shakespeare

William Shakespeare was born in 1564, and died in 1616. In the course of his fifty-two years he wrote some thirty-seven plays and a number of poems which have made him probably the most famous author in the world. His fame, and his continuing popularity with theatre-goers, have created a strong demand for details of his life. Biographical accounts of Shakespeare vary in length from a few lines crammed in at the start of a cheap edition of one of the plays to lavishly-illustrated full-length books. All these accounts, long or short, are based on four main ingredients. First, there is what might be called proven fact, one example of which is Shakespeare's baptism on 26 April 1564: parish records prove that this took place, and the fact cannot be argued with. Secondly, there are a large number of what might be called educated guesses, many of them based on years of research by scholars, and which whilst not totally beyond doubt are usually taken as being by and large correct. Thus the fact that there is a topical reference in Shakespeare's *Henry V* to a military expedition led by the Early of Essex suggests very strongly that the play must have been written after the start of the expedition, but before the return of its troops, which would place the play firmly as being written some time between 1588 and 1599. Thirdly, there is information based on the large number of traditions that have gathered round Shakespeare's name in the time since his death. Some of these traditions are worthy of serious consideration, some are pure fancy. The traditions that suggest Shakespeare acted relatively minor parts in his plays – Old Adam in *As You Like It*, the Ghost in *Hamlet*, and Time in *The Winter's Tale* – are either simply persistent theatrical traditions that no one has been able to trace to source, or reports collected at second and third hand from people who might have known Shakespeare. Fourthly, there is the category of pure guesswork, such as the idea that Shakespeare served as a soldier or lawyer during his life. There is nothing to stop the student reading, and enjoying, all four categories of information, but it is useful to know from which category an item is drawn.

It is sometimes stated that we know very little about Shakespeare. This is not true. A great deal more is known about Shakespeare than about any other dramatist of his time, with the exception of Ben Jonson

(1572–1637), and the fact that there is a great deal which is not known is merely typical of the age in which he lived – an age in which dramatists were not very highly thought of, and written records were few, unco-ordinated, and subject to loss and destruction over the years. What is true is that in terms of the modern interest in Shakespeare it is the wrong sort of information that has come down to us through the years. It is fascinating to know the number and ages of his children, but most modern critics and readers would gladly exchange this for details of when *Hamlet* was first performed, or what Shakespeare thought of his own plays.

John Shakespeare, William's father, was a prosperous glover and wool merchant, who probably dealt in other commodities as well. The town in which he lived, Stratford-upon-Avon, had its own prosperity assured by the land which surrounded it, then and now some of the richest and most fertile in England. John Shakespeare's choice of wife was in part a testimony to his rising social status: Mary Arden was a rich farmer's daughter, and when in 1552 she married John she brought along with her a rich dowry in land and ready money. Local records frequently reveal odd pieces of information that give some hint of the domestic details of life in sixteenth-century England, and thus we know that in the same year that they were married one John Shakespeare was fined twelve pence for failing to remove a dunghill from land which he owned.

The couple produced two daughters, both of whom died in infancy. William was born in 1564, and other children soon followed: Gilbert (1566–1612), Joan (1569–1646), Anne (1571–9), Richard (1574–1613), and Edmund (1580–1607). Of these, the youngest of William's brothers, Edmund, was the only one to make any attempt at a theatrical career. He was an actor in London, but died young at twenty-seven years of age. There is a tradition that Shakespeare knew very little Latin and Greek – at that time and for many years to follow the main and sometimes the only ingredient of a school syllabus – the result of his father being unable to afford the expense of educating his eldest son. If this is so it is difficult to reconcile with the clear successes John Shakespeare began to enjoy in the commercial and business world of Stratford and its neighbourhood. In marrying Mary Arden John Shakespeare had moved up a rung on the social ladder, and this was a movement that continued. He started to receive what would now be known as 'local government' appointments in 1556 when he became an ale-taster for Stratford, responsible for the price and quality of the bread and the beer offered to Stratford's two and a half thousand inhabitants. This sounds an enjoyable job; it was also essential in an age when there was no piped water supply, and most people (including children) out of necessity drank ale or beer, which would be rendered relatively pure by the brewing process. A succession of other jobs followed, leading to his appointment in 1565 as an alderman, a leading figure in local politics. The pinnacle of his career came in 1568, when he was appointed bailiff or mayor of Stratford. After this his career went into decline, for reasons we do not know. He was in financial trouble by the 1570s, and a warrant for his arrest was issued in 1573 for a debt of thirty pounds. By 1576 he was no longer attending council meetings, although his fellow councillors did not officially replace him as an alderman until much later, in 1587. In 1592 he was cited as being a non-attender at church, fearing that he would be arrested for debt if he went to a service. He died in 1601, his wife in 1608.

It is known that William Shakespeare was baptised on 26 April 1564. He was presumably born a few days earlier, and 23 April is usually given as the date of his birth; it gives a reasonable time before the baptism, it is St. George's day, and it is also the date on which he died. We know there was a school in Stratford in the time of William's youth, that it was staffed by a teacher and an usher or assistant teacher, and that William was eligible to attend it by virtue of his father's position. In the absence of any other information it is usually assumed that William attended the school and received at least some education. It is known that he married Anne Hathaway, eight years his senior, in 1582. She bore him their first child, Susanna, five months later. Those who have written on Shakespeare have differed widely in their reaction to the apparent fact that England's greatest author married in a hurry (by special licence) after having made his future wife pregnant out of wedlock. Some critics argue that by Elizabethan social convention the couple could have 'plighted their troth' before the actual marriage ceremony, and that if this had been done there would be no shame or disgrace in Anne's pregnancy. Other critics attempt to ignore the awkward dates, comment briefly in stiff-lipped disapproval; and others dwell rather too long on the business and draw up romantic scenarios in which the young, innocent Shakespeare is bewitched and finally trapped by the older and more experienced woman. If one can guess at the truth it is that Shakespeare had to marry Anne Hathaway, but managed to make a perfectly reasonable marriage out of the whole business. The twins Hamnet (1585–96) and Judith (1585–1662) were born shortly after Susanna.

There is firm evidence that Shakespeare was in London, writing plays and acting, in 1592. There is hardly any evidence at all for what he was doing between 1582 and 1592, and at no point in Shakespeare's life are the rumours stronger or more numerous. He was forced to leave Stratford as a result of falling into bad company and stealing some deer from a vengeful Sir Thomas Lucy of Charlecote; he rebelled at the prospect of being a glove merchant in Stratford for the rest of his life, and ran away to London; he became a sailor; a soldier; a lawyer; a medical student; a teacher; he joined a group of travelling players who had visited Stratford; he founded a thriving business holding the horses of those who had come to watch plays at London's new theatres . . . and so on. Whatever the truth, in 1592 Shakespeare was sufficiently well established in London to be the victim of an envious complaint from the dying dramatist Robert Greene (*c*. 1560–92). Greene referred to Shakespeare as an 'upstart', and his attack prompted a reply from another dramatist citing Shakespeare's honesty and skill as a writer. Shakespeare seems to have spent from approximately 1592 to 1610 living in lodgings in London, whilst steadily buying houses and property in Stratford and in London. At that time actors operated in companies, and Shakespeare seems to have written for at least three different companies until 1594. From that time on he became a member of a company known as The Lord Chamberlain's Men. This company was extremely successful, and was later allowed to call itself the King's Men, receiving royal patronage and being counted as members of the royal household. Shakespeare was clearly on the way to becoming a rich man, but his money did not come to him as a direct result of the plays he wrote, but rather from his position as an actor with a share in the profits of the company of actors of which he was a member. He seems to have moved back to Stratford in 1610, and to have stopped writing altogether in 1613. Again, rumours are plentiful: it has been written that he became a sick man, and was thus forced to retire to the country; there is the tantalising possibility that he may have viewed his plays and his whole involvement in the theatrical life of London simply as a way of making enough money to retire and live the life of a country gentleman in Stratford. He died in 1616, on 23 April. His will still exists. One tradition has it that he died of a fever contracted whilst drinking at a reunion with Ben Jonson.

The bare facts of Shakespeare's life are that he was born to prosperous parents and made his way to London in defiance of any family tradition, and once there became a successful and prosperous actor, dramatist, and businessman. He achieved as much fame in his own day as that particular age was prepared to grant to any dramatist, and retired whilst still comparatively young to live a life of properous retirement in his home town. He appears to have made very few enemies, and a number of good friends, during his life, and to have shown little or no concern for the publication of his own works. The bare details of his life – birth, marriage, death, involvement in law suits, purchases of land – are comparatively well documented; of his attitude to his work and art, his feelings about the theatre, his loves, his hates, and his philosophy of life we have nothing, except the lines he wrote in his plays, which may or may not be based on actual experience and personal feeling. Perhaps, after all, this is one of the biggest blessings, after his plays and poems, that Shakespeare has left to later generations, for the absence of personal detail about Shakespeare leaves the field clear for an uninterrupted view of the plays themselves.

The historical and social background

At first sight the differences between the modern age and Shakespeare's age can seem so pronounced as to be almost frightening, suggesting that it is impossible for someone to speak across the years to a present day audience. It is true that a huge number of things have changed since Shakespeare's day: what has not changed, and what still allows the plays to be seen and read with vast enjoyment across a wide range of cultures and nationalities, is human nature. Shakespeare's Hamlet wore a doublet and hose, had never heard of electricity or aspirin, and would have his teeth out without the benefit of anaesthetic. Despite these differences, Hamlet's mind, his moods, his feelings, and his thoughts are wholly and completely modern – or perhaps eternal. Shakespeare's characters may dress differently from us today, and even speak in a different way, but they think and feel exactly as human beings have done for five thousand years, and it is this ability to perceive what is lasting and eternal in human nature that gives Shakespeare his strength and his appeal to all audiences.

Some historians place the population of Elizabethan England at one-tenth or less of its present size. In London itself there were probably 150,000 inhabitants, unthinkably large to the average Elizabethan, almost ludicrously small to the modern Londoner, accustomed to sharing his city with twelve million other inhabitants. The small size of Queen Elizabeth's England was due in large part to the death rate. Mary Shakespeare's first two children died in infancy, a quarter of her family, and one of Shakespeare's brother's died whilst still young, as did Hamnet, Shakespeare's own son. There was virtually no medical care, as we know it, in Shakespeare's time. Plagues ravaged London with almost clockwork regularity, emptying the city and forcing the authorities to close the theatres for fear of spreading infection. Elizabethan ideas on hygiene and basic sanitation were either rudimentary or non-existent. In the middle of city streets ran an open gutter into which the night's urine, faeces, and waste were thrown, together with any other foul rubbish. This is the origin of the convention whereby a well-mannered man always walks on the outside of a lady: the outside position was the most likely to collect the contents of the chamber pot as it was emptied out of a window, and thus by taking this position the man was protecting the lady. The position was not quite as bad as it sounds, as the waste matter was collected by entrepreneurs and used as fertiliser, but it was bad enough. Water was drawn from wells that were often polluted, and it was safer to drink ale or beer, purified by the brewing process. Personal hygiene was rudimentary. Body lice were common, and without proper dental care even young people could carry on their breath the stink of rotting teeth: it is no accident that in Elizabethan literature, and earlier, 'sweet breath' is a major feature to recommend a lover. Bathing was infrequent when all water had to be heated on open fires. Little was known about the body and about proper medical care. There was no protection against a host of illnesses that have almost vanished from the most advanced countries nowadays, such as smallpox, cholera, and typhoid, with bubonic plague a major killer because of the absence of proper sewerage or hygiene.

However, the situation for an adult member of Elizabethan society was not as desperate as it might sound. The average life expectancy may have been only just over thirty years of age, but the figure is made so low by the large numbers of children who did not survive their first eighteen months or so of life. Those people who survived to adulthood stood at least a reasonable chance of reaching a ripe old age, and there was no shortage of seventy year-olds in Shakespeare's time. The real differences between the ages are more diffuse and less obvious than the basic figures of life and death might suggest.

Elizabethan society was rigidly and strictly divided into social classes, as discussed below, but there were other divisions which tend not to appear in the history books. Probably some eighty per cent of the population in Elizabeth's England were living in rural environments, with the majority of these being directly concerned in and with the production of food. Travel was strictly limited, and most peasants or lowly rural farm workers would never go beyond twenty or so miles of the village of their birth during their whole lifetime. Even Queen Elizabeth, a much-travelled monarch, never went further than the Midlands of England. Starvation over the winter period was a very real possibility for many of the populace; a large degree of self-sufficiency in food was necessary since almost no produce could be imported out of season as today, and the most highly-prized cooks were those who could invent rich sauces to cover the taste of salted-down beef, often kept in casks for six months or more, rancid, foul, and worm-ridden by the time it came to be broached.

Roads, by modern standards, were mere tracks. Well into the eighteenth century potholes on country roads were deep enough to drown the unwary traveller, and even major roads were frequently impassable when heavy rain had reduced them to mere mud baths. By the time of Queen Elizabeth London's atmosphere was already starting to cause concern. Coal from the North East of England could be transported relatively easily to London by sea, and its heavy use by

Londoners was starting to produce the famous London smog that did not finally vanish until legislation in the 1950s allowed only the use of 'smokeless' fuels in big cities. In London itself the River Thames dominated the city. It was a major transport route, in effect the biggest and best 'road' in the city, a source of water, an open sewer, and a thriving port for ships from all over Britain and Europe.

There were huge divisions of wealth throughout the kingdom. At the top, the King or Queen and the nobility lived lives of what was then vast luxury, whilst at the bottom of the social ladder the farm worker lived in primitive conditions that would be unthinkable for a civilised society today to impose on any of its members. The monarch was, in effect, a totalitarian dictator, and the key to power in the kingdom still lay in the acquisition of land. It was land and houses that Shakespeare brought to finance his retirement, and it was land and property that gave eligibility for election to Parliament, and almost any worthwhile office. The great land owners – the nobility and the few middle class families who had risen in the service of the crown – may have lived their lives at a level unimaginable to their poorer neighbours (a court lady's dress might take two years to make, and cost more money than a farm labourer and his family would see in the course of a whole lifetime), but 'Death the Leveller' took hold of rich and poor alike, and the noble families could fall by rebellion against the crown with extreme rapidity, to face an ignominious death in public from the executioner's axe.

An Elizabethan was closer to nature in some respects than his modern counterpart – but not in the sense that this phrase is sometimes used nowadays, implying a completely harmonious and happy relationship between mankind and the natural environment in which he lives. An Elizabethan was close to nature because he had no option. He rose with the sun and went to bed at nightfall, because candles and oil lights were both expensive and inefficient. If it suddenly became colder he shivered, rather than simply turning up the central heating. Those who have gone on camping holidays will know how in the space of a few days one's awareness of the weather is heightened to a significant extent, because one is so much more dependent on it. If it rained the Elizabethan got wet, for he had no nylon or PVC waterproofs to protect himself, and no hot bath to climb into to take away the cold and the damp. Winter to an Elizabethan was a serious business, requiring planning and skill for survival. No dryers cured the grain for the Elizabethan farmer, and if it rained when the harvest was due, or the grain rotted, then people went hungry.

Despite all this the temptation to dismiss Elizabethan England as a primitive society, and pat ourselves on the back for being so far advanced, should be firmly resisted, for the best of all reasons: it is wrong. An Elizabethan nobleman, and perhaps some gentlemen, would be expected to know the immensely detailed court etiquette, be well versed in classical and other literature, and have knowledge of the science and medicine of the day. He would be expected to be able to fight, to lead his forces in battle for his monarch, to sing, to write poetry, and to dance, as well as having a passing knowledge of the law, history, farming, accountancy, and languages. The various courts of Europe were havens for the very best in art, music, and literature, and we owe the survival of so many fine works of art to the patronage and support provided by royalty and the noble families of Europe. No one who has seen Burleigh House, near Stamford in Lincolnshire, is likely to accuse the Elizabethans of being primitive. Indeed, the typical Elizabethan country house, with its subtle use of red brick, its long mullioned windows, its high chimneys and its E-shape layout, is unsurpassed in any age for its beauty, elegance, and practicality. In other areas, too, the Elizabethans were a match for the modern age. In a deceptively simple manner they saw the whole Universe as a linked entity, a unity in which it is impossible to affect one area without also affecting others. A modern ecologist could be forgiven for thinking that it was the twentieth century that invented the idea that every item in the natural world is interdependent, but the Elizabethans were there long before. There is no doubt that the modern age is more advanced in terms of command of the physical sciences, and that existence in Elizabethan times was harsher, more dangerous, and more painful. But there is no doubt also that Elizabethans laughed and cried at much the same things as we do nowadays, and for much the same reasons, and that in their rigidly divided society those of the top end at least were the equal of any of our contemporaries in their artistic and cultural awareness.

In historical and political terms the reign of Queen Elizabeth used to be seen as a 'golden age' in English history, a view which is almost certainly unfounded. It is also wise to remember that Shakespeare lived under two monarchs, Queen Elizabeth I (1533–1603) and James I (1566–1625), and that Shakespeare is arguably as much a 'Jacobean' writer as an 'Elizabethan' one. Queen Elizabeth came to the throne of England after a period of immense upheaval, caused largely by the action of her father, Henry VIII (1491–1547), who had come to the throne in 1509. At Henry VIII's accession, England was a full member of the Roman Catholic Church, and Henry himself married to a staunch Catholic, Katherine of Aragon (1485–1536). However, Katherine produced no male heir for Henry, and he began to tire of her, particularly as he fell hotly in love with Lady Anne Boleyn. Henry hoped that the Roman Catholic church would annul his marriage to Katherine, the only form of divorce possible in those days outside death, and he persuaded himself that he had right (and, no doubt, God) on his side. However, the Pope was unable to face the tide of hostility that annulment would produce from European royal families, and refused. The result was that a furious and impassioned Henry declared himself the Supreme Head of the English Church, thus replacing the Pope, declared his marriage invalid in his new capacity as Head of the Church, and proceeded to marry Anne Boleyn. She bore him a female child, Elizabeth, but was executed soon afterwards, in theory for adultery. Henry subsequently took four more wives, but could only produce one male child, the sickly Edward, who was to reign briefly after his father.

The take-over of the Church was a major rebellion. In the aftermath the vast wealth and property of the religious orders were grabbed by the crown, and either kept or sold off to the highest bidders. The excuse offered for this act was the corruption that had overtaken the monasteries and priories of England; wealth had undoubtedly caused corruption, and scandals were frequent, but greed was the driving force behind the dissolution of the monasteries, and this sudden influx of land onto the market – much of which went into the hands of the new middle classes who thereafter came to be a force to be reckoned with in a society where power and land ownership were inseparable – had wide-ranging social, political, and economic repercussions. Possibly the breach between England and the Roman Catholic church could still have been bridged if the guardians of the new king, the nine-year-old Edward VI (1538–53), had not sought and succeeded in changing the actual form of church service used in England. Henry VIII had changed the ownership of the Church; Edward's reign changed its nature, into that of a genuinely Protestant as distinct from Catholic religion. Confusion was added to confusion when Edward died in 1553; for the next five years the new Queen, Mary I (1516–58), the daughter of Katherine of Aragon and married to the Catholic King of Spain, tried to put the clock back and return English religion to the hands of Pope. Heretics (those who refused to accept Roman Catholicism) were burnt at the stake; Mary had to defend the Tower of London against attack by rebels and supporters of Protestantism; and the average inhabitant of the country must have wondered where the chaos, change, and suffering would all end. When Mary died, the only descendent of Henry VIII was Elizabeth, despite rival claimants: England held its breath to see what path Elizabeth, daughter of a Protestant mother, would follow.

Elizabeth was very shrewd: she saw how fragile her own hold was over her kingdom (apart from anything else England's two previous Queens, Matilda (1103–67) and Mary had produced disastrous reigns) and she realised that most of Europe was hostile to Protestant England. She announced that she did not wish a window into mens' souls, and whilst enforcing Protestant observance in her kingdom did so with comparatively little fierceness, at least during the early years. With hindsight, Elizabeth's reign can appear as a golden age; in practice, it was a worrying time for all who could think more than a few months ahead. Elizabeth was a woman, and therefore expected to get married if only to produce an heir to the throne. If she married it might be expected that her husband would become ruler in all but name. A marriage to an English nobleman could split the nobility into warring and jealous factions, whilst a marriage to a foreign prince would be unpopular with a nation forced into isolation by Henry's Reformation, and with a grudge against Europe as a result. No marriage would mean no heir, and that was worry enough for a nation with a civil war only a few years behind it. Equally worrying was the threat from Europe, and in particular from Spain. Philip of Spain had a claim to the English throne through Mary, and the Pope had declared it no sin for anyone, internally or externally, to overthrow the English monarchy and replace it by a Catholic one. For practical and moral reasons Spain seemed set to mount an invasion of England.

By the end of Elizabeth's reign the situation was only slightly different. She had not married, and there was therefore no direct heir. The nearest in line to the throne was James VI of Scotland (1566–1625), and the problem here was two-fold: James's mother was Mary Queen of Scots, who had been executed in England on Elizabeth's orders for plotting against her; and James was King of Scotland, perhaps England's oldest and bitterest enemy. No one knew whether James would be allowed to take over the throne, and what his attitude would be towards the country that had killed his mother and been the bitterest enemy of his homeland. As it happened, the transition was remarkably easy, especially in view of James's attributes. He was a stunted man whose tongue was too large for his mouth, causing him to slobber; he had phobic fear of bared steel (whilst he was in his mother's womb she had witnessed a man who may have been her lover, Rizzio, stabbed to death with over fifty incisions); he had a virtually maniacal dislike of tobacco; he had a fondness for interrogating witches himself; and he also tended to form strong relationships with attractive young men . . .

This brief history helps to explain some of the worries and uncertainties that are visible in Shakespeare's plays, and in particular the overriding concern with kingship, the rights of succession, and political power. Government to Shakespeare and his fellows was not merely a question of how high the taxes were; it could mean, quite literally, the difference between life or death, if the monarch of the day was unable to stop either rebellion from within or invasion from without.

There is also another side to the coin. Under Elizabeth England prospered. In the absence of civil war or a major European war it began to grow in confidence and its middle classes, the trading part of the nation, prospered. The early excitement and spirit of adventure which is visible under Elizabeth did not last for long, but we still hold as symbolic of her reign the great Elizabethan sailors such as Sir Francis Drake (1545–96) and Sir Walter Raleigh (1552–1618), who sailed to the corners of the earth and in their puny boats, and, at least when they were lucky enough to meet a Spanish treasure ship, brought back vast wealth to their sponsors. Elizabeth herself sponsored such voyages. In an age when the monarch was expected to pay for many of the expenses of government out of her own income, Elizabeth was desperate for money, and not always too scrupulous about where it came from. The rise of the middle classes (merchants, clerks, lawyers, civil servants) also brought its problems to the monarchy, who needed their goodwill in Parliament to raise anything like significant quantities of money. Parliament had to be silenced by Elizabeth with increasing frequency, as it began to feel its muscles and test its strength against the monarchy. In under fifty years after the death of Elizabeth that same Parliament would order the execution of a reigning monarch, and attempt to run the country as a republic.

Shakespeare's theatre

Early models and the development of the theatre

In 1576 a building known simply as The Theatre was erected in Shoreditch, an area just outside the official boundaries of the City of London. This venture, the first time that a purpose-built theatre had been erected in England, was so successful that within a year two more theatres had been built. The originator of the building and its financier was one James Burbage (d.1597) whose son Richard Burbage (c.1567–1619) was to become a shareholder and leading actor in Shakespeare's own company of actors. Burbage's venture sprang from a number of factors. The performing of plays was unpopular with the authorities in the City of London: they believed that large gatherings such as were found at the plays, which were already popular, could lead to riot and disorder (compare this with the attitude of authorities to soccer hooliganism nowadays, and you will find that there are surprising similarities), and the plague spread easily in areas where large numbers of people sat or stood in close proximity to each other. The actors had a habit of behaving in 'unsuitable' ways – by seeming, for instance, to criticise leading personalities of the day, and being irreverent towards both people and institutions. However, London had spread beyond its legal boundaries by the latter part of the sixteenth century, and no doubt the actors themselves were pressing for a building designed round their needs. Certainly Burbage seemed aware that a purpose-built theatre, rather than the inns, in which most plays had previously been performed, would attract a better class of person. A theatre audience goes there to see a play; an audience in an inn can be there for a variety of reasons, by no means all of which make them suitable theatre-goers.

The building of The Theatre is a convenient date from which to start the growth of the Elizabethan and Jacobean theatrical tradition; it is perhaps too convenient, because it tends with its neatness to obscure the fact that plays had been in evidence for many years prior to 1576, and that the Elizabethan and Jacobean theatrical revolution did not happen overnight. It was a coming-together of many influences, some of which had their roots back in the Middle Ages. Some of these influences are listed below.

1. *Itinerant actors and the first theatres*
There may have been no theatres in England before 1576 (that is, no purpose-built theatres), but acting there certainly was. Wandering groups of actors would arrive in towns and villages, set up a rough stage with a few poles and some planks, and perform coarse comedies, or acts that would remind a modern audience more of circus than of serious drama. These wandering groups of performers left a number of legacies to the Elizabethans. Indeed, if the rumour that Shakespeare was recruited by one of these groups in Stratford is true, then all later generations owe the existence of England's greatest dramatist to one of these groups. Allowing for this possibility, the greatest proven legacy that the wandering troupes left was in the design of the theatre itself. The group of actors would often set up their stage in the yard of an inn or pub. It was an obvious spot. Most inns were built on three sides of a square, with a large entrance for horses, carts, and wagons forming the fourth side of the square. There was therefore a large floor space for audience directly in front of the back wall, and the more elegant inhabitants of the town could see the play in the inn yard from the rooms that would ring the stage area on three sides. There might be galleries or balconies available for the actors in the wall that they were acting against. The inn itself would have its regulars as a basic audience, with the addition of anyone attracted there for the show itself. Refreshment was readily available, as was lodging for the actors if the landlord chose to reward the company for the increase in his business that way. The stage itself would be set up at the end of the inn yard, thrusting out into the audience. When asked to build a theatre in London, the designer turned, logically enough, to the venue which had probably seen more plays performed than any other, which was the yard of a typical Elizabethan inn. It would seem that the first theatres were in effect little more than re-creations of such yards. The word 'seem' has to be emphasised here. Hardly any contemporary drawings of Elizabethan theatres survive, and there is no certainty that such as there are have total accuracy of detail. There is documentary evidence, in particular the

builder's contract for the Fortune Theatre, drawn up in 1600, but informative as this is it leaves considerable gaps in our knowledge. From all the evidence, and from years of scholarly research, it would seem that the basic details of the Elizabethan theatre were these:

(*a*) It was small – perhaps only eighty feet square in its external dimensions – but the stage area appears to have occupied almost half the internal floor space.

(*b*) The stage was an 'apron stage', jutting out into the audience so that they surrounded it on three sides. It appears that seats actually on the stage were available for the audience at a number of theatres, if not all.

(*c*) There was a large open area in front of the stage known as the pit, where the poorer people stood in the open air to watch the performance. The stage itself had a canopy over it to protect it against the elements, often with 'the heavens' (stars and other devices) painted on it.

(*d*) There was a curtained recess at the back of the stage, used for many purposes. In Shakespeare's plays these included the witches' den in *Macbeth*, and the area in which Hermione's 'statue' was kept in *The Winter's Tale*.

(*e*) There was a gallery or balcony at the back of the stage. This could be the battlements of Flint Castle in Shakespeare's *Richard II*, the balcony from which Juliet speaks in *Romeo and Juliet*, or the vantage point from which the Ghost speaks in *Hamlet*. As with the curtained recess the balcony could be a convenient place for large numbers of people to die, as they could remove themselves after the event without necessarily being seen by the audience – a significant point when there was no curtain to block off the audience's view of the stage.

In 1598 The Theatre was dismantled and reconstructed on the south side of the Thames, where it became known as the Globe Theatre. It was here that many of Shakespeare's plays were first performed. By 1608, however, Shakespeare's company had moved to Blackfriar's Theatre, an indoor space with much more sophisticated stage machinery than was available at the Globe although they appear to have continued to perform here as well. The change is visible in plays from Shakespeare's later years, which require more elaborate staging effects, such as a storm at sea and the descent of the gods, in *The Tempest* and *Cymbeline* respectively.

2. *Mystery plays*

The medieval church seems to have turned to drama, after a fashion, quite early on in the Middle Ages, by allowing the performance of representations of certain scenes from the Bible. It was an obvious way to bring the Bible alive to villagers who were unable to read, and who were simple in their responses. These early plays were massively popular, and the Church appears to have become worried that it was

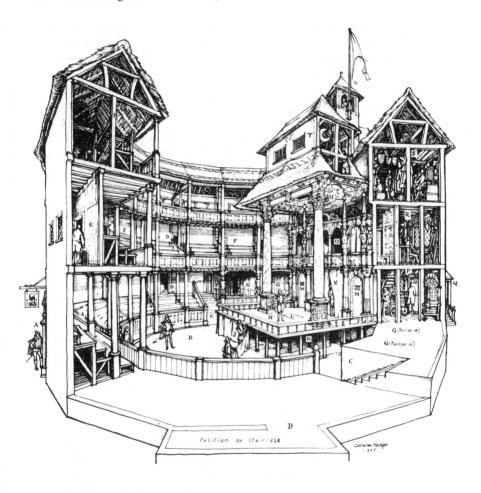

A CONJECTURAL RECONSTRUCTION OF THE INTERIOR OF THE GLOBE PLAYHOUSE

AA Main entrance
 B The Yard
CC Entrances to lowest gallery
 D Entrance to staircase and upper galleries
 E Corridor serving the different sections of the middle gallery
 F Middle gallery ('Twopenny Rooms')
 G 'Gentlemen's Rooms' or 'Lords' Rooms'
 H The stage
 J The hanging being put up round the stage
 K The 'Hell' under the stage
 L The stage trap, leading down to the Hell
MM Stage doors

N Curtained 'place behind the stage'
O Gallery above the stage, used as required sometimes by musicians, sometimes by spectators, and often as part of the play
P Back-stage area (the tiring-house)
Q Tiring-house door
R Dressing-rooms
S Wardrobe and storage
T The hut housing the machine for lowering enthroned gods, etc., to the stage
U The 'Heavens'
W Hoisting the playhouse flag

drama and not religion that was drawing people to see the plays and act in them. In the event, the plays seem to have been taken over by the medieval guilds. The guilds are sometimes described as similar to modern trade unions, but the analogy is not exact. They were a cross between a union and a modern professional association, responsible for regulating standards within a given trade, supervising training and apprenticeship schemes, and generally attempting to ensure that a given trade and those who practised it were both thriving. The guilds had considerable resources at their disposal, both financially and in terms of manpower, and were the natural legatees of the religious plays. There was a trade interest in the business of acting as well: a short play on the subject of Noah's Ark allowed the ship builders guild to extol the virtues of their trade and its product, and no doubt the opportunity was taken to boost the image of whichever guild was involved in the production of a play.

The plays themselves became vast, complex, and expensive ventures. They became known as 'mystery' plays because each guild tended to refer to its own trade or craft as a mystery (for that matter it is still a mystery to most of us how ships are built or how rope is made). The plays were on Biblical themes, often with a number of playlets on each topic, ranging from the Creation to the Crucifixion. A different guild might be responsible for each short play. The plays were mounted on wide carts, and performed at several spots on a grand tour of a town or district. Thus by staying in the one spot a resident could hope to see the complete sequence brought round to him. Because of the number of short plays they contain, the complete mystery play is sometimes referred to as a 'cycle'. The York, Wakefield, and Chester cycles of mystery plays have survived to the present day, and can still occasionally be seen in performance. Effects were often spectacular in these plays, with directions calling for a Hell's mouth complete with real fire, thunder and rain.

It is not possible to quantify the effect these plays had on Elizabethan drama in the same way that the main impact of the travelling players can be assessed, save to say that their popularity and spectacle encouraged a taste for drama that can only have contributed to the popularity of drama in Shakespeare's time.

3. Morality plays

The mystery plays had their greatest popularity in the fourteenth and early fifteenth centuries. In certain areas at least they then began to be supplanted by the morality plays, of which perhaps *Everyman* is today the most famous. Unlike the mystery plays, morality plays were not based specifically on Bible stories, but were allegories, showing good and evil battling for man's soul. Characters such as Anger, Vice, and Greed gave much opportunity for broad comedy, as well as for moral instruction. The morality plays tended to be performed indoors in halls, and to have a rather more select audience. Occasionally they were performed by professionals. Falstaff, perhaps Shakespeare's most famous comic character, is said to derive from the Vice figure in the old morality plays.

4. *Interludes*
These were learned plays written for a select audience by scholars and clergymen, often in Greek and Latin, and usually acted by amateurs. They too dealt in moral themes, often in the form of a debate. These plays may have done as much to influence the design of indoor theatre such as that at Blackfriars as the travelling players did to influence the first open theatres.

It is tempting to see a direct chronological progression in English drama, from religious playlets to mystery plays, and from thence onto morality plays and interludes. As ever, things were not quite as simple as that. What can be said is that drama in its various forms was becoming increasingly popular and increasingly sophisticated.

There were two further influences on Elizabethan drama that are worth mentioning. The first of these is the classical author Seneca (*c.*4BC–AD65), a Roman whose tragedies were known and widely-read in Shakespeare's time. They were written to be read rather than performed, with dialogue more like formal speech than everyday dialogue, and are full of bloody and horrific events. The theme is usually revenge, the ending a complete bloodbath, and ghosts and other strange events pepper the action. The gore, the violence, the ghosts, and the gloom of Seneca's plays caught the Elizabethan imagination, and may have been instrumental in starting the whole fashion for 'revenge drama' in Elizabethan times, typified by the works of Christopher Marlowe (1564–93), and plays such as *The Revenger's Tragedy*, probably by Cyril Tourneur (1575–1626), and probably first performed around 1606. The violence of Seneca can also be seen in plays by John Webster (*c.*1580–1634) such as *The White Devil* (1612) and *The Duchess of Malfi* (1614). Shakespeare's own *Titus Andronicus* shows the influence of Seneca, and his *Hamlet* is one of the finest treatments in literature of the revenge theme. However, Seneca was not merely all violence and blood, though he certainly was more pessimistic than at least some of the earlier Greek authors. The Stoic virtues of endurance and patience feature largely in Seneca; in a world of cruelty, suffering, and misery, and where these are normal and to be expected, the capacity to endure becomes an essential element in the survival of humanity, and perhaps the only way that human nature can triumph over a Fate or Destiny that seems certain always to be cruel, unfair, and almost random in the suffering it inflicts. Shakespeare's *King Lear* deals masterfully with the theme of endurance, and a character such as Brutus in *Julius Caesar* may owe much to the influence of Seneca.

A second major influence was Niccolo Machiavelli (1469–1527). Machiavelli was a civil servant and politician in what was then the independent state of Florence. In 1512 Florence was defeated and Machiavelli was imprisoned, tortured, and eventually exiled. In his exile he wrote *The Prince* (1513), in which he stated that strong government was the only method of securing a happy and stable society, but that people were fundamentally greedy, envious, ambitious – and even evil. To survive against such people and so ensure strong and stable government the ruler had to be able to match people at their own game, and be able to lie, use force, cheat, and deceive in order to maintain his power. The good ruler, of course, had at the same time to pretend that he was above all evil, and leading a blameless life. Machiavelli's theories were not as horrific as the above summary makes them sound: his philosophy that the end justifies the means was merely writing down what had undoubtedly been good practice for all astute politicians and rulers for years, but it caused vast shock, horror, and outrage when it was read. Elizabethan dramatists seemed gripped by this doctrine of power politics, although the effects of this interest were often far removed from anything Machiavelli had said. The cynical, totally unscrupulous villain who rejoices in his wickedness with every sign of satisfaction (Edmund in *King Lear*, Richard in *Richard III*, Iago in *Othello*) seems to have been inspired by Machiavelli. Shakespeare's history plays also frequently make the point that a good man does not always make a good King, and that kingship often requires a man to sacrifice both a part of his free will and some of his more humane qualities.

These are some of the literary and dramatic influences that paved the way for Shakespeare, and perhaps influenced the form of his work. A wider knowledge of them than this book can offer is strongly advised for any serious student of Shakespeare, partly because many of the works mentioned above, such as the plays of Seneca or *Everyman*, are worth reading in their own right, and partly because they help to give a sense of perspective to the student's reading of Shakespeare's work.

The plays in performance

It was a very different world and a very different theatre that saw the first performances of Shakespeare's plays, but not so different that the plays cannot be performed to stunning effect nowadays.

The design of Shakespeare's theatre has already been discussed. Some estimates place the maximum capacity of a theatre such as the Globe as high as two thousand, but the actual space inside the theatre was small, and the actors close to their audience. Plays were performed in the afternoons, usually starting at about 2.0 p.m. The early theatres had to rely on natural light, and the start of the performance was signified by three trumpet blasts, a flag having been hoisted earlier to show that a play was to be performed that day. The audience ranged from the rich and privileged, high up in their private boxes, to the rabble standing in the pit, the 'groundlings'. These latter cracked nuts and drank their ale during the performance, and not infrequently rioted or engaged in drunken brawls. They clapped when they liked what they saw or heard, and hissed or mewed when they disliked it, in extreme cases hurling rotten fruit and abuse at the stage and the actors. The Elizabethan theatre was a noisy place. A black hanging at the back of the stage told the audience they were to see a tragedy, a coloured or embroidered one a comedy or lighter play. Once started, the play would be over in something like two hours. There were no act or scene divisions, these having been added into our modern texts by modern editors; instead, the next scene would take place as soon as the actors for the previous one left the stage. The plays were acted on the bare stage, and there was no 'set' in the modern sense. If the audience needed to know where a scene was taking place, the actors told them, working the information into the dialogue. Thus in Shakespeare's *Twelfth Night* the heroine's first words are to ask where she is, and she is speedily answered by a convenient sea captain. Weather conditions, where necessary, are similarly conveyed ('So fair and foul a day I have not seen'), and if a scene is meant to be taking place in darkness servants or the characters themselves walk on stage clutching burning torches, even though the actual theatre was bathed in the light of afternoon. The actors appear to have spoken fast, and their gestures and expressions were more stylised and conventional than those seen in the modern theatre. Elizabethan acting seems to have been less naturalistic. If the stage was bare of scenery, then the same was not true of 'props' (properties): cauldrons, dragons' and devils' heads all appear on Elizabethan inventories of items owned and used by the theatres. Costumes were rich, extravagant, and expensive, seeming to take a disproportionate amount of a company's budget, but no doubt adding to the air of authenticity of the plays and providing a rich spectacle. Processions were common in Elizabethan plays, where King, Queen, and the whole paraphernalia of royalty would march across the stage to the accompaniment of trumpet blasts and other music. The entry of any royal character always had an accompaniment of trumpets – ignored or treated with embarrassment in the modern theatre, but clearly revelled in by the Elizabethans – and there was much music in the plays. Some modern authorities think there may even have been almost continual music, in the manner of background music in a modern film. Wind, thunder, and cannons firing could be simulated on stage, although in the case of the cannons they used the real thing rather than any imitation. During a performance of one of Shakespeare's history plays one of the Globe theatre's cannons fired burning wadding into the thatched roof of the theatre, with the result that within an hour the theatre had completely burnt down. Even if the plays were set in the past there was little attempt at historical accuracy: Shakespeare introduces chiming clocks to the Rome of *Julius Caesar*, and as far as we are aware actors wore contemporary, Elizabethan costume, rather than the dress of the period in which the play was set. For the director wishing to present a Shakespearian play as close to the original as possible the major features are that the Elizabethan actor was close to his audience and in an intimate relationship with them, not cut off by the proscenium arch or 'picture frame' theatre that became popular at the turn of the seventeenth century; and setting was created by words rather than by physical means, and the words and the action moved fast, without break. A director (itself a position with no equivalent, as far as we know, in the Eizabethan theatre) who wished to be purist might seek also to banish women from the stage. Morality and convention dictated that all female parts in Elizabethan plays had to be acted by young men, it being considered improper for women to appear on the stage. This has resulted in modern audiences being subjected to some appalling experiences, in the name of historical accuracy. The squawking thirteen or fourteen-year-old of today is a world apart from the 'boys' who would have acted the female roles in Shakespeare's plays: they were rigorously trained from a very early age to take these parts, and it should also be remembered that harsher living conditions meant that boys reached puberty much later in Elizabethan times. A seventeen or eighteen-year-old in Shakespeare's time might still have an unbroken voice, whereas the thought of not having reaching sexual maturity by eighteen would bring a blush of embarrassment to a modern adolescent.

The theatre was based round the various 'Companies' of actors that existed in these times. The original groups of travelling or itinerant actors were worthy of the respect of no one unless they could claim the patronage of a rich lord or noble. By calling themselves The Lord Chamberlain's Men, Shakespeare's company of actors were harking back to the days when the Lord Chamberlain would actually have entertainers living in each of his households, and though the members of Shakespeare's company were no longer tied to such an extent to the Lord Chamberlain, their use of his name both expressed a special responsibility to him, and suggested that in a vague sense the company were legitimate and operating under the protection of the Lord Chamberlain. In practice Shakespeare's company would have performed to a bewildering variety of audiences, and in a bewildering variety of settings. They might be called one evening to present a play before the

Queen or King, the next to the groundlings and apprentice boys in the Globe. Socially, it must have been a very confusing existence.

The company itself was organised much along the lines of a modern business operation. Actors and other assistants were paid for their services, but at the top were a relatively small group of 'sharers' who in effect ran the company and took a share in its profits – or losses. The demand for new plays was ferocious. Long runs of plays were unknown, and the system as it then operated was similar to the modern repertory system, but speeded up some ten or fifteen times. One Elizabethan company, The Admiral's Men, performed eleven different plays in a space of twenty-three days, and there is no reason to think this was unusual. By modern standards plays must have been grossly under-rehearsed, but the actors were professional, well-trained, and perhaps more used to improvisation than their modern counterparts. Of course, plays were revived later if they had been a success on their initial performance, but the Elizabethan actor must have had to carry an impressive number of different plays in his head.

The written word

The texts of the plays presented, if they were a success, were very valuable property. With no law of copyright to protect authors, there were as few written copies of the play as possible. Rival companies would go to great lengths to obtain the text of successful plays from other companies. It is possible that they even sat people in the audience of a play to take the words down in shorthand. It is certain that they bribed actors to write down their own parts, and whatever they could remember of other people's parts, and would then rush into production a 'pirate' version of the play, claiming, no doubt, that it was the original. Plays were published in the lifetime of an author, but only when they could not be kept from other companies, or were out of date. There is often no certainty that these versions were the original that the author wrote, many of them being pirate, inaccurate texts.

The only texts Shakespeare seems to have personally supervised for publication were two poems, *Venus and Adonis* (1593) and *The Rape of Lucrece* (1594). Nineteen other plays by Shakespeare were printed and published during his lifetime, either in 'bad quartos' ('quarto' simply refers to the way the pages were folded in the book) which appear to have been taken from what actors could remember of their parts, or in 'good quartos' in which the text seems to have been taken either from Shakespeare's own writing, or a copy of it. Virtually all of his plays and poems appeared in the First Folio, printed and published in 1623 by colleagues after his death, and there were subsequent folio editions in 1632, 1663 and 1685. It is by no means certain that what is seen and heard on stage in a modern production of Shakespeare is what he actually wrote. The original folios and quartos were based on a variety of sources, by no means all of them accurate; Elizabethan printing was eccentric; and in an age when it was by no means unusual for writers to collaborate, there are undoubtedly lines and speeches which are not by Shakespeare in his plays, and lines and speeches which are by him in plays by other authors. There is no literary manuscript which is known for certain to be in Shakespeare's handwriting. The modern texts used by most students may perhaps have modernised spelling and punctuation, be divided up into act and scene divisions which did not appear in the original, and will also contain sections that are pure guesswork on the part of the editor.

Shakespeare's plays are now performed all over the world by a wide variety of players. Shakespeare, however, wrote his plays for a very specific group of actors, whose strengths and weaknesses he knew well, and was most probably quite limited in what he was able to write by the potential of the actors he had at his disposal in the company. Thus it is almost certain that the same actor played Shadow in *Henry IV Part 2*, Sir Andrew Aguecheek in *Twelfth Night*, Slender in *The Merry Wives of Windsor*, Le Beau in *As You Like It*, and possibly Osric in *Hamlet*: all these parts require a very thin actor, skilled at portraying the fool or silly gentleman part. Early Fool parts were written for the famous clown Will Kempe (*fl.*1600), who as with most Elizabethan clowns was an entertainer, singer, and dancer as much as an actor, and the later Fool parts for the more melancholy Robert Armin (*fl.*1610); Armin's stamp is on Feste, Jaques, and the Fool in *King Lear*. The great tragic parts were first acted by Richard Burbage.

The Elizabethan world

Every period in history has its own culture, a collection of ideas about the world, how it works, and people's place in it. In some respects the Elizabethans looked at their world very differently from the average citizen of today. Their views were based on a mixture of ancient and classical writers such as Plato and Aristotle, the Old and New Testaments of the Bible, and the perceptions of the Middle Ages, with a dash of the Renaissance, or new learning, that was sweeping Europe. There are a large number of allusions in Shakespeare's plays that might easily be missed, or misunderstood, nowadays. Just as a modern writer would mention electricity or motor cars without feeling the need to explain them, so Shakespeare could talk about the music of the Spheres and the four elements and assume that his contemporary audience knew what he meant without explanation. The student needs to know about comparatively few of these, the major ones of which are listed below.

Order

The Elizabethans lived a very precarious existence, at least in physical terms, and were much less able to influence, change, or alter their physical environment than we are. In effect, they were much more at the mercy of the elements. In their political world there was no effective and efficient transport system, with the result that local barons and lords could rule as kings, far removed from the centre of authority, and effectively out of its reach. Slack or weak government did not only threaten more tax or a bad balance of payments, but also families robbed and left to starve to death with no recourse to law, civil war in which whole towns could be reduced to ashes, and total economic collapse for the regions affected. The uncertainties of Elizabethan political life – a Queen with no direct heir, the threat from Spain, the response of a Scottish King to England – have all been mentioned. The result was that Elizabethans felt themselves much closer to chaos and anarchy than might be the case today. To counter this fear, they had a firm and fixed concept in order, which was both a belief and a need.

The Elizabethans believed that everything in the world had its natural mode of working, and its natural place in the scheme of things. Before the creation of mankind and the world there had been Chaos – an actual physical state in which no one particle of matter was able to bond to another, and all things were in a permanent state of anarchic conflict and hostility. God then imposed his own law on matter and formed the world out of Chaos. As everything was created by God, the whole cosmos was like a carefully linked and complex machine created and kept working by the one Being. The world is always on the brink of dissolution and a return to Chaos; it is order that keeps everything working and in its place, and it is order that staves off dissolution. Order can be seen in many things, such as a rigid class-structure in which everyone has his or her fixed place or the love and loyalty that a son owes to his father. It can also be seen on a wider and larger scale in the heavens with the planets following their fixed courses, night following day, and the progress of the four seasons, all of which are manifestations of order. The most commonly-quoted expression of this belief in and need for order in Shakespeare's work is a speech in his play *Troilus and Cressida*. The speech begins with a prime image of disorder. The planets are kept in their proper orbits by God's will. The author imagines them breaking free from their proper paths and careering randomly through the Universe, causing death and destruction. Since in Elizabethan thinking the planets influence events on Earth, so Earth will suffer too:

> But when the planets
> In evil mixture to disorder wander,

What plagues and what portents, what mutiny,
What raging of the sea, shaking of earth,
Commotion in the winds! Frights, changes, horrors,
Divert and crack, rend and deracinate,
The unity of married calm of states
Quite from their fixture ! . . .

(I.3.94–101)

Shakespeare, after having drawn this horrific picture of destruction,
then talks about degree, everyone having his or her own place in society.
Degree is the social equivalent of order. Without it society will
disintegrate, civilisation become impossible. Schools will vanish and all
learning, trade will be disrupted, inheritance and family succession will
vanish, no one will respect old people, and government will be
impossible:

Oh, when degree is shak'd,
Which is the ladder of all high designs,
The enterprise is sick! How could communities,
Degrees in schools, and brotherhoods in cities,
Peaceful commerce from dividable shores,
The primogenity and due of birth,
Prerogative of age, crowns, sceptres, laurels,
But by degree, stand in authentic place?

(I.3.101–8)

The climax of the speech then follows, an appalling vision of Chaos
where Nature, unrestrained by order, rises up against itself and destroys
the world, where madmen and lunatics have authority over the sane, and
sons kill their fathers:

Take but degree away, untune that string,
And hark, what discord follows! Each thing melts
In mere oppugnancy: the bounded waters
Should lift their bosoms higher than the shores,
And make a sop of all this solid globe;
Strength should be lord of imbecility,
And the rude son should strike his father dead.

(I.3.109–15)

Order is seen as the frame upon which the fabric of civilised life is woven.
Our own age has discovered many secrets of chemistry, physics, biology,
and a host of related sciences, each of which has its laws. In this sense the
Elizabethans anticipated our concept of the structure of the world, but
for them the prime necessity was not for an understanding of how the
laws work, but for the very laws themselves to exist.

Hierarchy

One aspect of the belief in order was that everything was ranked and had its place in a hierarchical structure which had God at the top and the lowest mineral at the bottom. A phrase coined to describe this Elizabethan outlook is the 'chain of being', in which everything that lives or was created is seen as being like a link in a vast chain. Of course the Elizabethans did not really believe that there was a huge chain stretching from heaven to earth, but they used this picture to symbolise and represent their view of how the world worked and was arranged. The image of a chain is very useful, implying as it does that everything is linked, just as one link in a chain is joined to a link above it and a link below it, and so suggesting how nothing can happen in isolation. Take out a link in a chain and the chain collapses; hit a link and the whole chain shudders.

There were six leading links or classes of links in this chain of creation. The highest was, of course, God, the source of everything. Under him was the next class, the angels, themselves divided into nine groups – Seraphs, Cherubs, Thrones, Dominations, Virtues, Powers, Principalities, Archangels, and Angels. Thus the highest form of angel was a Seraph, the lowliest an actual angel. The third class was that of Man, who had the four qualities of existence, life, feeling, and understanding. The Emperor was the highest being in this class, the beggar or physically and mentally disabled the lowest. Fourthly, there was the so-called Sensitive class, who had existence, life, and feeling. These were divided into three sub-sections, those of the higher animals, animals, and mere creatures. Fifthly, there was the Vegetative class, which had existence and life, and which would include flowers and plants. Finally, at the bottom, came the inanimate class, which had mere existence without life, sensitivity, or understanding, and which included metals, liquids, rocks, and minerals. Certain references in Shakespeare's plays take on a new meaning when this hierarchy is understood. Fire, eagles, dolphins, whales, and gold are all at the top of their respective classes, and so are powerful images of strength, purity and goodness, just as a reference to a cur implies the lowest of the low in the dog world. Macbeth's speech to the two murderers in the play *Macbeth*, when he is discussing the murder of Banquo with them, contains a multitude of references to curs and animals at the bottom of their respective classes, and thus implies that the murderers themselves are contemptible (III.1.91–107). There are, of course, similarities between a chain and a ladder, and the image used by the Elizabethans does contain within it the potential for upward movement.

The Universe

Elizabethan ideas about science may seem very strange to modern understanding, and they were in fact being challenged by the new learning of the Renaissance. The idea was still current that the Universe consisted of a number of concentric spheres, possibly nine in number. God inhabited the outermost sphere, the *primum mobile*, from which all the others took their movement. The two innermost spheres were those of the moon and of earth. This is a double-edged concept. Looked at in one light it makes the Earth the centre of a Universe, but in another it makes it the cess-pit, where all the dregs gather. The Elizabethans believed that everything in the created world was made up of four elements, Earth, Air, Fire, and Water. In their pure state, or when mixed properly, these were immortal. When God created Adam and then Eve as the founders of humanity, all on Earth was in this pure state, including Adam and Eve, and there was no illness, disease, or death. Then Adam and Eve fell from grace by disobeying God, and this, the Fall, brought *mutability* into the sphere of Earth. This was a state where the elements were either impure or mixed in wrong proportions, and so were subject to decay, death and sickness. This only applied to the area enclosed by the sphere of the moon. Above this all was still pure, and a circle of ether sealed off Earth from the other spheres, like a sterilising layer. Meteors were thought to be fragments of fiery ether collapsing into Earth's sphere. The spheres were supposed to produce a divine and marvellous music as they revolved, though this could not be heard by human ears.

The Elizabethans also believed in correspondences. As everything had been created by the one Being, so the same pattern would, logically, emerge throughout creation. Thus they saw links between the state and the human body; the king's equivalent was the brain, the guiding and controlling force; ministers were eyes and ears, and the humble peasant the feet, and so on. The four elements also had their equivalents in the human body, known as the four humours: choler, blood, phlegm, and melancholy. If they were mixed in perfect proportion inside the body then the person would be healthy and have a good personality, but most humans had an imperfect mix. A person's personality would be dictated by his humours; for example a man with too much choler in him would be bad-tempered and aggressive.

The Elizabethans believed that the stars exerted an influence on the world and events within it, although Edmund in *King Lear* pours scorn on this idea, saying that people blame the influence of stars for events because they are too stupid, idle, or incompetent to dominate events themselves. Again, before the Fall the stars were so balanced in their influence as to have no evil or bad effects, but this altered with the Fall.

Despite their belief in astrology the Elizabethans were also very religious, at least in the sense that very few Elizabethans would have failed to believe in the existence of a Christian God. Failure to attend a Church service once a week was a punishable offence in law, and, in an age when England's enemies were largely the Roman Catholic countries of Europe, politics and religion were closely linked.

Kingship

The Elizabethan attitude to kingship and monarchy also differed in several major respects from the attitude nowadays towards those who have responsibility for government. There was a religious element in kingship, as well as a political one, and the concept of the 'divine right of kings' needs to be understood before many of the comments and attitudes found in Shakespeare's history plays can be understood. This concept stated that it was God and God alone who was responsible for the appointment of a person to kingship, operating as he did through the hereditary principle: the King held his office from God, and was not appointed by other humans. Therefore any attempt to remove a King or to 'usurp' him was not merely a crime against human law, but a crime against God, and an attempt to decide something that only God could decide. Usurpation or the murder of a monarch is therefore a huge sin and crime against Nature in Shakespeare. The idea that the King or Queen held his or her office from God was carefully fostered by monarchs through the ages, not least of all Elizabeth I, for the obvious reason that it was an added protection against rebellion and gave moral justification for their attempts to resist any attack on their throne. There was also a very practical element in the principle, in that once it was shown that a reigning monarch could be removed from the throne, a precedent would be created that could easily lead to chaos and civil war. Shakespeare's support for properly-constituted monarchs – even if they are weak at the job of government – is support for stability as well as for kingship.

Reading list

Some of the more significant documentary evidence both on Shakespeare and his theatre is given in J. B. Harrison, *Introducing Shakespeare*, Penguin Books, Harmondsworth, 1966. In particular this book prints the fascinating Henslowe and Alleyn contract for a new theatre, dated 1600, and the text of Shakespeare's will. The classic reference work for thoughts on the Elizabethan outlook and ways of thought is E. M. W. Tillyard, *The Elizabethan World Picture*, Penguin Books, Harmondsworth, 1972. For those who require rather more detail of the background to Shakespeare, such as the classical sources for his work, and a straightforward, no-frills academic approach, M. W. Badawi, *Background to Shakespeare*, Macmillan, London, 1981, is the best buy; for pure enjoyment, *Introducing Shakespeare* has illustrations and a rather more relaxed style.

As with Shakespeare's life, it is essential to reach a proper sense of balance with background information. There is enough information readily available to see the student through all but the trickiest paths of Shakespeare, and the Select Bibliography at the end of this Handbook gives details of recommended further reading. Time spent on acquiring background information is rarely wasted, but the reading of texts and Shakespeare's own words must always be viewed as the priority.

APPROXIMATE DATES OF SHAKESPEARE'S PLAYS

Before 1592   *Henry VI Part 2*
Henry VI Part 3
Henry VI Part 1

?1592–1593   *The Comedy of Errors*
Richard III

1593–1595   *Titus Andronicus*
The Taming of the Shrew
The Two Gentlemen of Verona
Love's Labour's Lost

1595–1596   *Romeo and Juliet*
Richard II
A Midsummer Night's Dream

1596–1598   *King John*
The Merchant of Venice
Henry IV Part 1
Henry IV Part 2

1598–1600   *Much Ado About Nothing*
Henry V
Julius Caesar
As You Like It
Twelfth Night

1600–1602   *Troilus and Cressida*
Hamlet
The Merry Wives of Windsor

1602–1606   *All's Well That Ends Well*
Othello
Measure for Measure
King Lear
Macbeth

1606–1609   *Antony and Cleopatra*
Timon of Athens
Pericles
Coriolanus

1609–1610   *Cymbeline*

1610–1613   *The Winter's Tale*
The Tempest
Henry VIII

Part 2

A general view of Shakespeare's works

The plays

Any list of Shakespeare's plays with dates can give the misleading impression that we know when they were written. However, exhaustive research has established the general order, even if exact dates may not be correct (see table opposite).

Shakespeare's work can be divided neatly (perhaps too neatly) into the early plays, comedies and histories, tragedies and problem plays or problem comedies, and romance plays, with a roughly chronological development along these lines being visible in his work. It is also tempting to see in this categorisation a development and maturing of attitudes as well: experimentation in the early plays; examination of society in terms of love and relationships (the comedies) and politics (the histories); examination of the individual and the supernatural forces pitted against him (the tragedies); attempts to reconcile the comic, historic, and tragic outlooks into one dramatic unity (the problem comedies or problem plays); and final success in this reconciliation with the romance comedies, which reflect the experience, thoughts and lessons of all the earlier types of play. Rarely, of course, do authors choose to develop so logically and conveniently for critics, and so neat a division of Shakespeare's work can never be wholly true and accurate. If it were, he would not have written *The Merry Wives of Windsor*, an innocuous comedy, in the same year as *Hamlet*, a major tragedy. However, a critic such as the nineteenth-century Edward Dowden (1843–1913) has received a great deal of undeserved scorn for his 'four period doctrine', in which he divided the work of Shakespeare into, first, the 'workshop' period, when he was experimenting; secondly, the 'in the world' period, when he was revelling in human life and writing the happy comedies and the history plays; thirdly, the 'Out of the depths' period of the great tragedies and problem plays; and fourthly, the 'on the heights' period where romance rules and tragedy, comedy, and history are all combined. Dowden was sentimental in his approach, and not objective or detached enough for modern taste, but this is merely the surface layer of his thesis. There *is* a development over the course of

Shakespeare's work, and it does follow broadly the pattern set out by Dowden. What cannot be established is any link between the events in Shakespeare's life and this sequence of development in his work, partly because for any author such links are always of dubious validity, and partly because there is insufficient firm evidence about Shakespeare's life anyway.

The significance and usefulness of knowing something about the broad pattern of Shakespeare's work, as well as knowing about an individual play, cannot be overstated. When archaeologists dig up some ancient weapon or artefact and photograph it a marked measure will also be shown on the photograph, because without this reference point it would be impossible to estimate the size of the object seen. The same is true of Shakespeare. Both the strengths and weaknesses of, say, *Hamlet* can be much more effectively seen by the student who has something with which to compare the play, something sufficiently similar to provide an comparison but different enough to highlight the unique features of *Hamlet*: *King Lear*, *Macbeth*, and *Othello* provide this magnificently. Knowledge of other plays tells the student what to look out for when reading a play in a similar vein or mould and gives a sense of perspective that is invaluable, particularly when a syllabus or course demands claustrophobic study of only one or two plays.

The early plays

Shakespeare's early plays can be thought of as including all the plays in the table on p. 34 up to and including *A Midsummer Night's Dream*, although other authorities would have the group end with *Love's Labour's Lost*. As a group name, 'early plays' tends to suggest plays which are best forgotten about, whereas in reality many of these plays are still performed and enjoyed. The three *Henry VI* plays are not in this category, and a performance of any of them anywhere is usually sufficient to make headline news. Shakespeare does not have control of his language or plot in these plays, at least to nowhere near the same extent as in his more mature work. *The Comedy of Errors* has an intricate plot featuring two identical twins, and, like *The Two Gentlemen of Verona*, is a relatively straightforward and superficial comedy. *Richard III* is part history play, part tragedy, and part comedy. It is historically completely inaccurate in its portrayal of Richard III, but as Queen Elizabeth's great-grandfather took Richard's crown by force it would have been tactless for Shakespeare to show Richard as anything other than a villain. Thus, Richard is seen as the hunchbacked, evil demon of England, revelling in his wickedness and shameless in his confession of it to the audience. *Titus Andronicus* is a tragedy and a blood bath. *The Taming of the Shrew* is a comedy telling the story of Kate, a loudmouthed, vicious-tongued, and spiteful girl who is finally tamed and made into a good wife by Petruchio; although it has been made into a film several times it is now out of favour with women's rights groups, presenting as it does a traditional view of women's subservience to man. *Love's Labour's Lost* is a sophisticated and gentle comedy about love, probably written for performance at court.

The early plays have many of the features that typify Shakespeare's maturer work – fine verse and poetry, insight into human nature, exciting or intriguing narrative, a vast sense of comic enjoyment, an unerringly accurate eye for the detail of human behaviour and personality – but they tend to present them intermittently, or in varying proportion. The verse can be clumsy, or simply go on for too long, and plots can become too intricate or out of control. The plays lie off the beaten track of most examination syllabuses, and are sometimes subject to patronising comment by examination students. One recent example is the comment 'There is not much wrong with Shakespeare's early plays . . .' At all costs avoid patronising Shakespeare; the tone of lofty condescension adopted by the student above might just be acceptable from someone with forty years of good literary criticism behind him, or a dramatist with a string of successes to his name, but it is not acceptable from someone whose knowledge does not run to having read all the early plays. There is a great deal right with the early plays, as witnessed by the fact that they are still performed regularly nearly four hundred years after the death of their author, and if they have suffered it is not because they are bad, but because their author went on to things that were even better.

The comedies

The term comedy originally meant merely a play with a happy ending, as distinct from a tragedy with its unhappy ending. The modern definition of comedy is more biased towards laughter, and this can cause some confusion when a student first turns to a Shakespearian comedy. Shakespeare's comedies are funny, and the make audiences laugh, but they do not only do that. They can have very serious elements in their themes and plot, and often concern themselves with some of the weaker aspects of human nature. This explanation is possibly only necessary for those brought up on a diet of filmed television comedy, with maniac laughter from a tape or cassette surfacing every few seconds on the sound track, and comedy taken to mean that at no time must anything serious take place or be mentioned to the audience, unless it is to be instantly deflated or mocked. Good comedy has always had a serious element in it. The circus clown is funny, but also often a pathetic figure, someone for whom things never go right, and someone for whom life is permanently out of control. Much humour derives from potentially serious situations where people demean themselves or make themselves look ridiculous – the man whose trousers fall down in public, or the person who slips on a banana skin are classic examples. Many successful films or television serials of a comic nature have been based on situations of desperate seriousness. The British series *Steptoe and Son* had at its heart an old man unscrupulously hanging on to his son and refusing to let him leave home or have a life independent of his father. The American film and television series *M*A*S*H* centred upon the activities of the emergency medical services in wartime Korea. A film such as *Butch Cassidy and the Sundance Kid* draws humour from two gangsters permanently under threat of death. Shakespeare's best known comic character (who, incidentally, appears for the most part in the *history* plays, not the comedies) is obscenely fat, a robber, liar, braggart, cheat, diseased, drunk, and totally without moral scruple or any feeling except selfishness. Thus comedy is not merely laughter: in practice all good comedy has had a marked vein of seriousness in it.

Shakespeare's comedies fit this pattern exactly. Just as there are generally held to be four 'great' tragedies, so Shakespeare's comic output is dominated by four plays: *Twelfth Night*, *As You Like It*, *A Midsummer Night's Dream*, and *Much Ado About Nothing*. Each play is different, but each has a number of shared features. Each concentrates on a small section of a specific society, usually the ruling or upper classes of a named country – Illyria in *Twelfth Night*, England in *As You Like It*, Thebes in *A Midsummer Night's Dream*, and Messina in *Much Ado About Nothing*. The leading characters are frequently misguided or at fault in some way, but by means of a love affair of one sort or another they are allowed to find their way out of their weaknesses happily, and with no major ill effects. However, not all the characters are allowed to escape in this manner. There is usually a character in the play who is left outside the 'magic circle' of lovers at the end of the play, someone who is unable to change, learn, or be redeemed, and who as a result cannot achieve final and lasting happiness based on self-knowledge and a true knowledge of the world. Thus Orsino in *Twelfth Night* is not really in love, but merely forcing himself into a belief that he is for his own selfish purposes, but he is allowed to find and marry the right person, Viola, despite his mistake. Malvolio, on the other hand, is too steeped in vanity and self-deception to be brought to his senses, and ends the play shamed, unredeemed, and ruined. The happiness of the other characters at the end of the comedies is given flavour and sharpness by the realisation, brought on by characters such as Malvolio, that things do not always end happily. The audience is made to value happiness by being given a taste of unhappiness: not enough to spoil the dish, merely enough to make its flavour welcome.

The key to the thematic content of the comedies is self-knowledge. The characters frequently have a false image of themselves, and, as a result, fail totally to see the truth behind other people's characters. It would need only a slight twist of plot for most of Shakespeare's comedies to turn into tragedies: the heroine dies at the altar after having been falsely accused of unfaithfulness by her fiancé – at least this is what for a moment appears to have happened in *Much Ado About Nothing*. However, the atmosphere of a comedy is manipulated so that whilst violent or gloomy events stimulate the audience they never really feel that an unhappy ending is possible or likely. This is the sort of trick that sounds easy when written down in a work of criticism, but which in practice requires a most delicate balancing act from the author. The happiness at the end of a comedy is worthless and empty unless it can be shown that misery and unhappiness could really have come about. Enough harshness has to be injected into the play to give it this feeling, to make it credible (few audiences believe in worlds where only good things happen, however much they might want to), and to provide narrative tension and suspense; but if the mixture becomes too strong the comedy will be soured, and the audience will hang awkwardly between two opposed emotions. To an extent this is what happens in the later 'problem comedies', where the action seems to be tragic but the ending is happy, and the two elements are never reconciled. The same principle, in reverse, can be applied to the tragedies: the violent and tragic action is relieved by a measure of comedy, but never enough to deflect the play from its main purpose. Just as a sombre element in a comedy can highlight and emphasise the comedy, so a comic element in a tragedy (the Fool in *King Lear* is an example) makes the tragedy richer and more strongly felt.

Discussion about the serious element in the comedies can tend to obscure the basic fact about them: that they are very funny. Their humour takes many forms. The Fool or Clown parts in the comedies tend to be of two distinct types. There is the 'low' comedy of characters such as Touchstone in *As You Like It* and Bottom in *A Midsummer Night's Dream*. These characters are lower class, often coarse and crude, but sometimes also skilled with words. At the other extreme stand Jaques in *As You Like It* and Feste in *Twelfth Night*, whose fooling is tinged with melancholy and bitterness, and who are altogether more intellectual and refined than the Touchstone and Bottom and other low characters. Word-play and punning is an essential source of humour, as, for example, in the convoluted speeches of Dogberry in *Much Ado About Nothing*, an arch-exponent of malapropisms, or the use of words in wholly unsuitable contexts.

Disguise is both a theme and a source of comedy. The most obvious form of disguise is the dressing-up of female characters in male clothing, as with Viola in *Twelfth Night* and Rosalind in *As You Like It*. A disguise of this nature allows for multiple ironies, and it is useful to remember that all female parts in Shakespeare's plays were played by boys. Disguise in another form is seen in the use of eavesdropping. One of the funniest sequences in Shakespeare is the orchard scene in *Twelfth Night*, in which the steward Malvolio unwittingly unburdens himself of all his private thoughts of love in the sight of his arch-enemies. Eavesdropping is also a significant feature in *Much Ado About Nothing*, and is the method by which the lovers are brought together.

Love, of course, is a major topic in the comedies, and every comedy has at least one love story at its centre. Love is not merely a method of arriving at a plot. Love signifies a unity and accord between man and woman, and the lovers can be made to represent a Universe in miniature, a Universe in which harmony, peace, and fruitful union have been achieved. The lovers in the comedies frequently start off either misunderstanding themselves and other people, or under threat from the world at large. The triumph of their love, and the multiple marriages that usually end a comedy, are symbolic as well as practical, showing how individuals can win through trouble and hardship to reach happiness and fulfilment. One of the aims of the comedies is to show people living harmoniously with one another in society, which is why the comedies operate in groups of characters, whilst the tragedies are dominated by one character. The tragedies end with peace having been achieved through death and purgation; the comedies end with peace having been achieved through people coming to terms with their own nature, and that of other people.

The comedies are, therefore, funny, but also searching in their analysis of human behaviour. In addition to plays already mentioned, *The Merchant of Venice* is known as a comedy, although only in the sense of it having a partially happy ending; its essentially serious concern is the conflict between the Jew Shylock and the commercial and social leaders of Venice. It does, however, have a courageous heroine, Portia, who fights for her lover in a man's world and wins. *The Merry Wives of Windsor* is also a comedy, and tradition has it that it was written for Queen Elizabeth I in order to satisfy her demand for another play with Falstaff in it.

The histories

Politics do appear in passing in the comedies. A banished Duke is at the centre of *As You Like It*, and the action in *Much Ado About Nothing* is preceded by a battle between the reigning Duke and his bastard brother. However, personalities and individuals dominate the comedies rather than nations and monarchs or rulers. This latter area is the concern of Shakespeare's history plays.

For all practical purposes there are four main plays in this group, the so-called 'second tetralogy': *Richard II, Henry IV Part 1, Henry IV Part 2*, and *Henry V*. Earlier chapters have suggested how vital the role of the monarch was in Elizabethan and Jacobean society, and the second tetralogy sets out to examine some of the more vexed issues of kingship, as well as illustrating some conventional points about it. The sequence opens with *Richard II*, a play that was apparently very popular in Shakespeare's own time. Richard is the rightful king; he has inherited the crown through his father, and his claim to it, legally and morally, is beyond question. He is also in some respects an attractive figure. He is a fluent and imaginative speaker, and clearly has reserves of courage and determination. He is not, however, a good king. He is unpredictable, has favourites, and he mishandles people, and in general fails on many of the counts against which he would be judged as an effective king. In particular he alienates one of his cousins, Bolingbroke, whom he banishes. Bolingbroke returns to England to claim back his position and his lands, and in the process of so doing finds himself deposing Richard and becoming king himself, almost without his wishing it. Bolingbroke, who is now Henry IV, is undoubtedly better suited to be King than Richard. He is shrewder, politically more skilful, and has far more in the way of authority and personal power than Richard – but Bolingbroke is not and never can be the rightful king, having taken the crown by force. *Richard II* ends with Henry in a fit of temper ordering the death of Richard, who dies bravely. The play illustrates the problems that arise when the rightful king does not have the necessary qualities to exercise his kingship effectively.

The two parts of *Henry IV* examine the other side of the coin. Henry IV has the personal qualities, but not the right. He has sinned in the eyes of God by taking the power of election to kingship into his human hands, whereas it should be left to God alone to make kings through the hereditary principle. As a result of Henry's illegal seizure of the throne, his reign is doomed from the start, his usurpation having let a cancer of rebellion into his kingdom. Henry is driven to his death by rebellion after rebellion, and the plays suggest that, however good the man, his reign cannot succeed if he does not have a right to the throne. There is a complex moral issue here in addition to the central one posed by Henry IV. He is in the wrong by having usurped and taken over the throne, but those who rebel against him during his reign are also wrong, and as guilty as Henry himself. This might seem odd when all the rebels are doing is trying to remove from the throne a man who should not be there in the first place, but the issue is the same. Man is not allowed to decide who shall be king under any circumstances, this task being God's and God's alone, and so even in attempting to remove a usurper rebels are at fault. This is a simple philosophy, and it does not always bear up under close scrutiny, but it was never intended for such scrutiny in the first place; the broad view is sufficient.

Richard II shows the chaos that results when a rightful but ineffective king rules, and *Henry IV Part 1* and *Henry IV Part 2* show the chaos and political sickness that results when an effective man without true title to the throne is in charge. The scene is clearly set for the ideal king to make his appearance, and Shakespeare produces him in the final play, *Henry V*. Henry (known as Hal in *Henry IV Part 1* and *Part 2*) has inherited the throne from his father, and so is not a usurper, and he also has the necessary qualities for a king. He is just, honourable, religious, militarily skilful, and powerful, fully aware of the responsibilities that he carries and prepared to put his country before his personal feelings and needs.

Broadly speaking, therefore, the second tetralogy plays discuss the questions of kingship and power, and specifically the requirements of and for the ideal king. However, the issue of what has to be sacrificed in order to achieve perfect kingship is also scrutinised, and this is where Falstaff enters the action. The young Prince Hal, who will eventually become Henry V, becomes friendly with Sir John Falstaff, a huge fat man based loosely on the Vice figure in the old Morality plays. Vice is dangerous, but also very attractive, and this is true of Falstaff. He is the last person on earth with whom the heir to the throne should be consorting, but he is amusing, witty, and free from any feelings of responsibility save towards himself and the satisfaction of his physical needs. Hal gives plenty of hints that he will reject Falstaff when the time is ripe, and Shakespeare progessively blackens Falstaff's character as his rejection comes nearer, presumably in order to soften the blow and avoid the audience's blaming Hal for doing what he has to do: Falstaff is anarchy, and the ideal king (or for that matter any king at all) cannot have anarchy at his elbow as he tries to govern. There has been, however, a persistent feeling amongst some critics and theatre audiences that the price Hal has to pay in order to become the ideal king is too great, and that in sacrificing and rejecting Falstaff he is turning himself into an automaton, a machine-like being who does everything right except retaining his warmth and humanity – in other words, that the price for perfect kingship is too high in human terms. This is a view that is easy to hold in a country for which economic, political, and social survival does not depend on the good offices of the monarch; but, as we have seen, the Elizabethan would have had a very different view of these issues. The student must form his own understanding of the situation and its outcome; but for Shakespeare to have suggested that Hal should retain Falstaff and so ruin a kingdom would have been remarkable indeed. Much depends on the extent to which Henry V is shown to suffer and display human emotions whilst he is undertaking the duties of the King.

Whereas marriage is the final symbol in a comedy, and rebellion the symbol of a diseased kingdom, so military success is used as the symbol of a successful reign in *Henry V*, with Henry's victory over the French at Agincourt the climax of the play.

The tragedies

Shakespeare's tragedies are probably the best known of all his plays. He wrote a number of tragedies, but four in particular have become known throughout the world: *Hamlet*, *King Lear*, *Othello*, and *Macbeth*. Various attempts have been made to define tragedy, but there is no comprehensive effective definition. The classical writer Aristotle (384–322BC) attempted a definition of tragedy in his *Poetics* (330BC), and this is often used as a base from which to define tragedy. However, it was not accurate even of the drama of Aristotle's own time, and it is even more out of keeping with later forms of tragedy. Never the less, some of Aristotle's tenets are still useful in helping us to come to a definition of Shakespearian tragedy, or perhaps more usefully a feeling for its essential elements. Aristotle stated that the tragic hero was someone who was neither exceptionally evil nor exceptionally good. This tragic hero begins the play as prosperous and happy, and is high-born, usually a king or aristocrat; he is moved from happiness to misery and eventual death through some fault or weakness on his part, the so-called 'tragic flaw'. The effect of tragedy in Aristotle's view was to arouse the emotions of pity and fear, and then to purge them from the audience (and the play) by the action. Shakespeare's tragedies adhere to most of these principles – but certainly not all.

Macbeth, for example, can be seen as a tragedy of ambition – ambition is Macbeth's 'tragic flaw'. He begins the play as a noble figure: he has fought magnificently for his king, the saintly Duncan, against rebels. But he soon departs from the noble, Aristotelian model and becomes infected and debased by the evil of ambition which eventually reveals his essential weakness. The combination of three witches prophesying that he will be king, his wife prompting him to murder Duncan, and Duncan's decision to spend a night at Macbeth's castle at the very time when the pressure to murder Duncan is greatest proves too much for Macbeth. He kills Duncan, and then suffers agonies until he is finally killed by a nobleman whose family he massacred when he was king. As do the 'history plays' and *Hamlet* and *King Lear*, *Macbeth* confirms that usurpation is a major sin, punishable by turmoil for the country and death for the usurper.

The tragedies, however, are concerned with more than kingship and the state of the nation. The influences of non-human forces are felt strongly in *Macbeth*, *Hamlet*, and *King Lear*: there are the witches in

Macbeth, the ghost of Hamlet's father in *Hamlet,* and numerous references to Fate, Destiny, and the gods in *King Lear.* The comedies are self-contained in the sense that everything which happens derives from the characters which the audience see: in the tragedies there is a supernatural element, a feeling that the action is being played out and in some cases caused by forces or powers that come from beyond the pale of human activity, and greater in their power and influence than humanity. The force is evil in *Macbeth,* but in *Hamlet* and *King Lear* the precise nature of the force is never quite made clear.

Tragedy always ends with the death of the tragic hero. This, of course, is a major contrast with the comedies, although in both cases the final solution may be preceded by comparable realisation, on the part of the protagonists, of the flaws that have beset them. In *Twelfth Night* Duke Orsino fails at first to realise the true nature of his servant Viola. In *King Lear* Lear fails to realise the true nature of his three daughters, Cordelia, Goneril, and Regan. In the comedy Orsino is allowed to marry happily and revoke his early error. In the tragedy, Lear and all three daughters die, a country is invaded, and large numbers of innocent people die. In theory an ending which has at its centre the death of the tragic hero should be intensely sad, but a first-rate performance of a tragedy does not usually leave an audience in tears, for a number of reasons. As Aristotle claimed, tragedies arouse the emotions of pity and fear, and then purge them; at the end of a tragedy an audience can be drained of all emotion, so purged and emptied as to be incapable of any further response. It is also true that there can be a tremendous sense of uplift at the end of a tragedy. The tragic hero may have been destroyed, but the spirit and strength he has shown over the course of the action can reaffirm the audience's faith in human nature. The death of the tragic hero can also be a relief, an inevitable conclusion which puts an end to suffering, and thus is something to be welcomed by the audience which does not wish to see a character it admires suffer any more or be demeaned by seeking a dishonourable way out. A sense of waste, of something uniquely valuable being thrown away, is also a strong element in most Shakespearian tragedy.

It is tempting to see the tragedies as the story of man against the gods, doomed to failure in a fight against superior odds but showing the nobility of his nature in the course of the unequal struggle. It is in practice not so simple. The stature of Macbeth is rapidly corrupted by evil. The events in *King Lear* are horrific and appalling; a form of rough justice does operate in the play, as all the evil characters are killed, but a number of the good ones must die as well. Hamlet dies at the end of the play, but he has killed an old man, been responsible for the death of two ex-friends from University, and indirectly caused the death of his girl friend. In *Othello* the gods, fate, or destiny have little to say; Othello's enemies are a recognisable human character, Iago, and his own nature. It can be argued that Iago is a devil, and part supernatural, but he is not in the same category as the witches in *Macbeth* or the ghost of Old Hamlet. For this reason *Othello* is sometimes referred to as a 'domestic tragedy'. A strong feature of all the tragedies, however, is the sense of inevitability which drive the events portrayed towards their conclusion. In each of them a man is subjected to vast suffering and stress that strips and exposes the bare bones of his nature to the scrutiny of the audience, and an awareness of man's strengths as well as his weaknesses – if not his nobility in the Aristotelian sense – can emerge from this.

Each of the four great tragedies has its comic element, something which was totally outside Aristotle's analysis – Elizabethan tragedy was never 'pure' in the sense of only containing tragic material. The Fool in *King Lear* provides much bitter comedy, and the grave-diggers scene in *Hamlet* and the Porter scene in *Macbeth* provide low-life comic relief without ever allowing the audience to lose sight of the plays' main themes.

Despite these links and similarities between the tragedies there are also significant differences. *Macbeth* reads very well, with its emphasis on the supernatural, its single-minded concern with the battle between good and evil, and the grinding inevitability of its violent climax, but oddly enough it is probably the least successful of the four tragedies in performance. It is perhaps too single-minded in its concentration, failing to provide the audience with sufficient variety or relief – of all the tragedies *Macbeth* shows most clearly the battle between good and evil for a man's soul, and the play has even been seen as an allegory of the Fall of Man. In some respects Macbeth himself is a difficult character for an actor to develop, and the witch scenes are perhaps too fantastic for a modern audience to absorb seriously. Added to this, the play is the focus of superstition in the acting profession, and is considered unlucky.

Othello, on the other hand, is perhaps the least stimulating of the tragedies to read, but perhaps the one that is most often performed successfully. Its plot is more complex than that of *Macbeth*, concerning as it does the attempt of Iago, a soldier serving under the generalship of Othello, to destroy his leader, choosing to do so by persuading Othello that his wife has been unfaithful.

Hamlet is the most intriguing of the tragedies and certainly the most adaptable. Hamlet has been played as a towering military hero, a disaffected student, an aging revolutionary, and as all kinds of permutations in between these extremes. The play points to a feature in Shakespearian tragedy whereby the tragic hero is seen as more or less innocent, unaware of the harsh realities of life but too trusting or ignorant to remain untouched by evil. Perhaps one of the reasons for the success of *Hamlet* is its portrayal of an adolescent who suddenly faces the crushing realisation that life is neither as simple nor as pleasant as it seemed to be in youth.

King Lear is intellectually the most complex of the tragedies, and some critics have seen in its ending a doctrine of total nihilism, a rejection of all hope. Again the student must form his own conclusions, but the debate does draw attention to a central concept in tragedy, that of regeneration. Tragedy, and in particular Shakespearian tragedy, presents to the audience a world in miniature. At the outset this world is apparently functioning well, but after a few scenes it is seen to contain the seeds of its own destruction. Somehow evil is allowed into this world, usually by some action of the tragic hero. King Lear decides to divide his kingdom, and then banishes his daughter and the noble who most love him, and rewards the the two daughters who hold him at nothing. This action is sufficient to unleash a tide of evil into the world of the play, evil which is only purged and destroyed when it has consumed good and turned at last on itself in a frenzy of destruction. Macbeth decides to murder Duncan, and thus lets evil into the world of Scotland, with similar results to those in *King Lear*. Othello's unlocking of the door to evil probably comes when he banishes Cassio and takes Iago, his sworn though hidden enemy, as his lieutenant. Hamlet is unique in that the action that has let evil into the world of Elsinore and Denmark is not his own – it is the murder of his father by Hamlet's uncle Claudius, something for which Hamlet is not responsible.

After the initial onset of evil, events in all the tragedies follow a set pattern. The tragic hero is increasingly made to suffer, and the society portrayed in the tragedy increasingly infested and infected with evil. There comes a crisis in which evil is defeated, but only at terrible cost, a part of which is the death of the tragic hero himself. At the end of the play, with the stage littered with corpses, the action is declared closed and a new figure – or figures – takes over to run the newly purged and cleansed society, suggesting that the blood-letting has not been entirely in vain. All the four tragedies differ in some respects in this matter, but all conform to it in general terms.

It is thought that tragedy derived from religious or semi-religious ritual in its earliest form, and Shakespearian tragedy, whilst not religious in the strict sense of the word, does give the feeling of dealing with basic moral issues of significance to all societies, not merely the one represented in the play itself. If the comedies make points about certain aspects of the way humans live with each other, and the histories points about the political side of man's existence, then the tragedies look at man's relationship with his whole environment and the interplay of good and evil in his world.

It is difficult at first sight to see why *Antony and Cleopatra* is not included in the list of the great tragedies. It is partly a history play in the sense that its story concerns the battle for control of the Roman Empire, and distinguished by having two tragic protagonists, as does Shakespeare's other great tragedy of love, *Romeo and Juliet*. It is generally held to contain some of Shakespeare's finest poetry, although its plot may be hampered by an abundance of scenes in which not very much happens. *Julius Caesar* is an earlier 'Roman' tragedy, and is much loved by examiners. Its title is a misnomer to a certain extent, in that its tragic hero is Brutus, not Caesar. Care should be taken when reading *Antony and Cleopatra* and *Julius Caesar*; although in history the events narrated in both plays follow on from one another, these are very different plays, and the Antony who appears in *Julius Caesar* is a totally different character from that in *Antony and Cleopatra*.

The problem plays

The 'problem plays' are generally held to be *Measure for Measure, Troilus and Cressida*, and *All's Well That Ends Well*. These plays fall awkwardly between tragedy and comedy, and seem to be neither one thing nor the other. Perhaps this is best illustrated by reference to one particular play: *Measure for Measure*. Duke Vincentio feels that his country is becoming corrupted, and supposedly leaves it to his deputy, the saintly Angelo, to cure the state of its ills, while he goes away. A young man, Claudio, has made his fiancé pregnant, and is the first person to fall foul of the new strictness on moral matters that Angelo brings in. Claudio's fault is not seen by the audience as severe – he was shortly to marry the girl anyway – and so it is a shock when Angelo pronounces the death sentence on Claudio. As a last resort a plea is put to Claudio's sister, Isabella, to speak on her brother's behalf to Angelo. Isabella is about to take her final vows as a nun, and it is felt that her purity will make her appeal stronger. However, the supposedly pure and saintly Angelo starts to feel sexual desire when he speaks to Isabella. He promises her that her brother will be spared if she agrees to have intercourse with him – but at the same time orders Claudio's death.

So far the play seems entirely in keeping with the plot and mood of a tragedy. Then the tone of the play appears to change completely, with the re-appearance of the Duke, Vincentio. Isabella's capacity to exert mercy is tested to the full, Claudio is spared, and the eventual outcome is that Angelo is allowed to live, and Isabella marries the Duke. There is excitement in the play, tension, and a searching exploration of moral issues, out of which no-one emerges unscathed. The problem is that the play is too sombre to be comic, too comic to be tragic, and in many respects utterly confusing.

Troilus and Cressida is similarly dark grey in its tone. The characters are all flawed without ever reaching tragic stature, and nothing great or noble is allowed to appear without being subject to scathing demolition. There is much philosophical debate in the play which rarely leads anywhere, and the action is often slow. *All's Well That Ends Well* shows in detail the despicable behaviour of its 'hero' Bertram, and then asks its audience to agree happily to a marriage between Bertram and the heroine, Helena, who has won her husband by robbing him of his ring and getting herself pregnant by him without his knowledge. However, this latter play shows to an extent the folly of dismissing any of Shakespeare's work: the Royal Shakespeare Company's production of the play in the Barbican Theatre in 1982, directed by Trevor Nunn, was magical. In this, the play's apparently unpromising material was skilfully interpreted to show a Bertram who is simply an adolescent who wants to sow his wild oats, and a Helena who is head over heels in love with a young man who, she knows, will be able to return her love in the due course of time. (For further details of the staging of this production, see pp. 137–41).

The problem plays are perhaps most interesting for what they suggest about the development of Shakespeare's art and thought. It is almost as if having written in the comic, historic, and tragic modes he is trying for a form of play that will combine and blend all three modes into one, new form. If the problem plays are the experiments, then the fruits of experimentation can be found in *The Winter's Tale* and *The Tempest*.

The romance plays

It needs no great insight to perceive the similarities between the problem plays and a play such as *The Winter's Tale*. The latter is divided down the middle, into two halves separated by a space of fifteen years, and thus can be compared to *Measure for Measure* which also has two distinct halves, though not separated in time. The ending of the play is happy, with general reconciliation and marriage, but the first half of the play contains several deaths and a plot which could be entirely tragic, and indeed remains as such right until the end of the play. The difference is that the sombre and violent events of the first half of the play do not spoil or render incredible the regeneration that is found at the end. Mistakes have been made, lives have been lost and this is never ignored or overlooked, but it is also recognised that time can heal wounds, mistakes can be rectified, and life can return to normal after a major disturbance. The violence and misery in the play is poised between the extremes of comedy and tragedy; the play shows the regeneration that is typical of tragedy without the same focus on anguish that pays for it in tragedy.

The Winter's Tale is like a *pot pourri* of techniques and devices used in Shakespeare's other plays. The 'death' of Hermione and her later coming alive has strong similarities to *Much Ado About Nothing*; the sealing of the bond of reunion and regeneration by marriage is a standard feature of the comedies; and the jealous rage that prompts Leontes to wrong his wife is reminiscent of *Othello*. There are also fantastic elements in the play which strain at the edge of conventional reality. In another late play, *Cymbeline* (worth reading purely as an adventure story, and a sadly neglected work), this goes one stage further when the gods descend from the ceiling to sort out the mess the humans have got themselves into. It is, however, in Shakespeare's last great play, *The Tempest*, that the element of fantasy is taken to its extreme. In some respects *The Tempest* is the culmination of Shakespeare's art, in others a disappointment. It is studied in detail later in this Handbook, and for the moment all that is necessary is to remark that it contains elements of all Shakespeare's previous plays – comedies, histories, tragedies, and problem comedies – but is the same as none of them; it is as if Shakespeare had tried to pour all he knew and all he had learnt into this one play.

The sonnets

A sonnet is a poem of fourteen lines, and in the Shakespearian form it usually has a rhyme scheme of *abab, cdcd, efef, gg*, or sometimes *abba, cddc, effe, gg*. Shakespeare wrote one hundred and fifty-four published sonnets, and it seems probable that a great many of them were completed before 1600. These sonnets are justifiably famous; however, the well-worn phrase 'Shakespeare's Sonnets' tends to suggest a well-defined sonnet sequence written to order and with a unanimity of style and content. This is certainly not so. There is immense variety within the sonnets. Some are general, public, and formal, others are personal and emotionally highly charged. They range from bawdy to delicate, from lyrical to brash, from sententious to dramatically personal. The most famous sub-section of the sonnets concerns those which deal with the author's relationship with a friend, and the intrusion of the so-called 'dark lady' into this relationship. Attempts have been made to suggest that this sequence displays a homosexual relationship between author and friend, and equally strenuous denials of this are also in print. Various attempts have been made to discover the identity of the dark lady, ranging from the entertaining to the wholly ludicrous, but none have preached their line with total conviction. The sonnets exist as individual poems of marvellous strength and power. The are best read and pondered over by the individual; of all Shakespeare's work they lend themselves least readily to glossing by critics and easy answers.

Shakespeare's themes

Perhaps the most significant thing to realise about Shakespeare is that he did not write his plays in order to gain a doctorate in advanced philosophy. The student who attempts to analyse at great length the 'meaning' of Shakespeare's plays is likely to be making the mistake of overlooking the stagecraft, the entertainment, the comedy, the tragedy, the emotion, and the language of the plays.

A theme is an issue or a group of issues examined by an author; he may sometimes (but not always) reach a conclusion about the issue or issues at the end of the work. It can be all too easy to look at a Shakespeare play as if it were an Aesop's Fable – a neat little story written to illustrate some truth or other, with that truth carefully spelled out at the end. Nothing could be more inaccurate as a guide to the way Shakespeare wrote and presented his ideas in his plays.

Shakespeare tends to observe life as much as comment on it. Thus in a play such as *Antony and Cleopatra* the audience is shown a love affair which can be viewed in two different and apparently contradictory ways. The love between Antony and Cleopatra can be seen as mere lust, and Antony cast as a villain for wanting to throw away leadership to infatuation and for mere physical gratification; but it can also be seen as a love of such power and intensity that the world is worth nothing by the side of it, and so Antony may be justified in discarding the world and all it has to offer for the sake of this transcendental love. In the final count Shakespeare never really comes down on one side of the argument or the other. He shows that both attitudes can live side by side in the same people in the same relationship; a love affair can be sordid and uplifting at the same time, and it can combine seediness and magnificence. It is not Shakespeare's thematic conclusions that are the most striking thing in *Antony and Cleopatra*, but the accuracy with which he observes life, and the total honesty with which he puts down those observations. One of the reasons why Shakespeare has survived into the twentieth century is that conclusions about the meaning of life tend to alter from age to age, but the raw material of human nature on which all conclusions must be based tends to remain the same. By observing and recording, rather than forcing a conclusion on the audience, Shakespeare lets them form their own views.

Themes are therefore only one part of Shakespeare's work, but they are a vital part, and are probably going to be at the heart of a majority of questions asked in an examination. Surprisingly perhaps, Shakespeare's themes do not tend to be very startling in their thought and content. Many of them are conventional and conservative, and tend towards tried and trusted truths rather than new, revolutionary ways of looking at life.

Appearance and reality

This is the theme that is the most common of all in Shakespeare's plays. In a Shakespeare play there are often two worlds: the world of appearance and the world of reality. The world of appearance shows or contains what *seems* to be true, whereas the world of reality is what actually *is* true. Success as a fulfilled human being, and even one's hold on life, is often shown as depending on one's ability to distinguish appearance from reality. Thus in *King Lear*, Lear cannot distinguish between the appearance of loving him presented by his daughters Goneril and Regan, which in reality is mere flattery and hateful hypocrisy, and the true love held for him by his daughter Cordelia and his courtier Kent, which Lear interprets as opposition to his will. The result is death for Lear, and a society half-destroyed by the powers of evil which Lear's misjudgment unleashes into the world. As is often the case in the plays, the theme of appearance and reality in *King Lear* is largely concerned with people, and the difficult task of seeing who is true and who is false. A point made in *King Lear* and in many other plays is that the ability to distinguish between appearance and reality often depends on the person concerned having self-knowledge – an accurate and honest idea of his or her own character and weaknesses. Lear has a false image of himself, and as a result cannot hope to see clearly into the hearts and minds of those he meets and lives with. If you do not know who you are, Shakespeare seems to be saying, you cannot even begin to know who other people are, and judge them correctly. In a comedy such as *Twelfth Night* characters can lack self-knowledge, but are allowed to learn it and knowledge of others without enormous sacrifice. Orsino thinks he is in love, but in reality it is only the idea of being in love that he likes, and he has a totally false image of himself. Similarly Olivia thinks she can lock the world away, but underestimates her own need to live in the outside world, and be loved in it. Both characters are allowed to learn from their mistakes and to marry the right partners. If any conclusion can be drawn from the theme of appearance and reality it might be summarised as the need to come to an honest and accurate picture of the world in which we live as quickly as possible, and in particular to acquire self-knowledge, and hence accurate knowledge of other people, their character, and their motives.

Love

Love is a major theme in the plays. Love between the sexes has little part to play in the history plays; it tends either to be bawdy and coarse, as in Falstaff's relationship with the prostitute Doll Tearsheet, or clumsily comic in Henry V's wooing of Katherine of France. The love that matters in these plays is love of one's country or King. In the comedies love plays a major role, with the plots of the plays usually based on at least one, and more often two, love affairs. Good, healthy, and happy relationships usually end in marriage, and marriage is used as a symbol of harmony and happiness. The capacity to give and receive love is an essential ingredient of the hero or heroine in a comedy; the figures who have this most abundantly are the twins Viola and Sebastian in *Twelfth Night*, and Rosalind in *As You Like It*. Characters who lack the capacity to love, such as Malvolio in *Twelfth Night* or Don John in *Much Ado About Nothing*, are left as outsiders at the end of their respective plays, and not allowed into the final festivities of the comedy. In the tragedies love is often defenceless in the face of evil – Lady Macduff's love for her children cannot prevent their cruel deaths at the hands of Macbeth's murderers, Lear's love for Cordelia cannot prevent her death – but at the same time is shown as an immensely strong force, and possibly one which can survive even death. Love is the one anchor point of decency and wholesomeness in a cruel world. Shakespeare shows its strength and its value, but he can also show how that same strength can be a force for evil. When turned in the wrong direction by the evil of Iago, Othello's love for Desdemona dissolves the bounds of civilised behaviour, and the passion thus perverted and released leads to the death of Desdemona and Othello; Lady Macbeth's love for Macbeth is one reason why she argues him into the disastrous act of murdering Duncan, his king; Hamlet is at his most vicious and tortured when those he loves (his father, his mother, and Ophelia) either die, or appear to turn against him. In Shakespeare's plays love is the ability to commit oneself utterly to the care and service of another person or persons. It is shown as a major need of all humanity to give and receive such love (even the most evil characters such as Goneril and Regan fall in love); it is shown as something with immense powers of healing and reconciliation, as well as immense power for destruction if turned in on itself or mishandled. In *Romeo and Juliet* Shakespeare wrote one of the most famous love stories of all time; a rather more probing and wide-ranging analysis of a love affair is contained in *Antony and Cleopatra*. These are the flagships of the love theme in Shakespeare's plays, but there is hardly a vessel in the fleet which does not have something to say about love.

Kingship

Kingship as a theme occurs most obviously in the history plays, although with so many of the tragedies centred round courts and palaces it becomes to some extent a theme in these plays as well. The history plays and their attitude to kingship have already been referred to in the section above on Shakespeare's history plays, and the discussion that follows of *Henry IV Part 1* and *Henry IV Part 2* goes into detail about this theme. In summary it could be said that Shakespeare views kingship as semi-divine, something which humans cannot decide upon, and as something which was of the greatest possible significance to contemporary society and its well-being.

Good and evil

Hardly a book or play exists which does not have good and evil, and the conflict between them, somewhere in it. Divisions between good and evil are often fairly clear-cut in Shakespeare's plays. Villains such as Edmund in *King Lear* and Don John in *Much Ado About Nothing* announce clearly who and what they are at the outset of their respective plays. Evil people in Shakespeare's plays are utterly selfish and self-centred, and incapable of true love. They are frequently hypocrites, adept at disguising the true nature of their evil and thus able to fool the world into believing them. Good triumphs in the end but often only after considerable suffering has been inflicted on the world or the society portrayed, even to the extent of widespread death and destruction.

In Shakespeare's plays the outward attributes of good and evil are never completely clear-cut. Claudius, as the usurper in *Hamlet* is, in terms of what he has done, almost the most evil character of all the plays: he has murdered a king and his brother – the dual crime of regicide and fratricide. Yet Shakespeare can show how this man is a good ruler, and an efficient one, and can actually feel regret at what he has done, albeit not enough to repent and give up what he has gained by his evil. Edmund is thoroughly evil in *King Lear*, but he is also witty, amusing, and, to the audience at least, totally honest about his evil. Falstaff is evil in the sense that he is debauched, unscrupulous, and guilty of almost every crime under the sun, but he, too, is shown as attractive by Shakespeare, again partly because he makes no secret of this evil to the audience – and this absence of hypocrisy reduces the threat of the character and allows him to be attractive – and partly because Shakespeare is also illustrating here the oldest truth of all, that, as vice and evil are so common, they must by definition be attractive or else people would not indulge in them.

A distinction has to be made between evil characters and misguided characters: evil characters are prepared to destroy other people if by so doing they can achieve their own personal aims, whilst misguided characters are simply too stupid, dull, or bigoted to behave in an admirable manner. Malvolio is one example of a misguided, rather than an evil, character.

Zest for life and the passage of time

In several plays Shakespeare condemns people for being unaware of the real world and unwilling to live life to the full. Shakespeare knows as well as anyone the fearful pressure imposed on a person when someone they love dies. A period of mourning is right and proper, but when that period of mourning is extended beyond its natural span, as it is with Olivia in *Twelfth Night*, or when any character appears to want to hide away from the real world, as with Isabella in *Measure for Measure*, then that character is shown as being at fault. Life is there to be lived in Shakespeare's plays, and energy and enthusiasm count as major virtues. It is no accident that some of Shakespeare's most popular characters are the women in his plays who dress up as men, challenge convention, and go out and try to take the world by storm: Viola and Rosalind are two examples, but great praise is also given to characters such as Cordelia, who leads an army back to England to rescue her father, and Helena in *All's Well That Ends Well* who goes out against all the odds to win back her husband. Falstaff's zest for life is shown as a major attractive feature.

Heroes and heroines in Shakespeare know when to act, but also when to let time work its magic and leave things be. The power of time to heal, mend, and solve problems is often emphasised. This is best seen in a play such as *The Winter's Tale* where a tragic sequence of events is eventually allowed to heal and lead to reconciliation between the parties involved but not before fifteen years have gone by.

Destiny and Fate, stoicism and courage

The conventions of Shakespeare's day did not allow the mention of God in plays, or specific references to the deity. One way round this was to set plays in pagan times; reference to pagan gods was allowed. Another way was to refer to Destiny or Fate, meaning the controlling power in the Universe.

Destiny or Fate are themes seen most clearly in the tragedies. *Macbeth* gives a direct vision of the forces of evil at work in the Universe, in the shape of the three witches. *King Lear* contains a whole set of often contradictory remarks about the gods and Destiny; at varying times in the play the gods are seen as just, as utterly cruel and devoted to torturing mankind merely for amusement, or as not existing at all. Hamlet accepts that there is a power or force which controls human destiny, but the vision of it in the play is cloudy and obscure. Stoicism and courage then become themes in *Hamlet*, and in other plays. If a person cannot hope to understand the way in which life is governed the only logical response is to endure whatever life throws at one with the maximum fortitude and courage. It is not always possible to influence what will happen but it is possible to respond to it in a manner that is both admirable and dignified, and ensure that even if Fate, Destiny or the gods destroy one's physical existence they cannot break one's spirit. Just as Shakespeare admires those who take the bull by the horns and try to achieve things, so he admires those who can endure suffering and hardship without crumbling under its impact; weakness is never attractive in Shakespeare.

The theme of courage has another, if connected, aspect. Modern societies can view the capacity to fight and kill other humans with considerable nervousness; in Shakespeare's day, when a monarch might well have to lead his armies out to fight hand-to-hand with an enemy or invasion force, military skill and prowess were admirable, much in the way that skill at sports is valued nowadays. Fighting ability is usually seen as a virtue only when used in the cause of good, but none the less we can find ourselves admiring the courage of the evil Macbeth at the end of the play, when he is about to lose his life and all he has worked and plotted for. Military prowess as a virtue can be seen in very many Shakespearian characters: Antony in *Antony and Cleopatra*, Hamlet, Henry V, and Othello are merely a few examples.

Madness

Madness is present in many of Shakespeare's plays. In thematic terms it is a response to intolerable pressure. Weak characters become mad and die, as is the case with Ophelia; stronger characters, such as King Lear, profit from it and become true men only when their sins have been purged from them through the fire of madness. Madness can also be used as a defence, a screen behind which a character can hide and recuperate. This is the form madness takes with Edgar in *King Lear*, and with Hamlet, though in both cases it can be argued that at times the act of madness becomes real, even if only temporarily. Just as a wound shows physical hurt, so madness shows the extreme of mental hurt; like an amputation, madness can kill, but it can also cure.

Part 3

Critical introductions to selected plays

Hamlet

General points

Hamlet was written in about 1600/1, at the height of Shakespeare's creative powers. It is arguably the most popular and famous play ever written, and its hero seems to have exerted a huge fascination over theatre audiences of every age, race, colour, creed, and time.

Corruption: the play contains a great deal of corruption, sickness, and disease imagery. Some critics link this to the supposed decline of the Elizabethan 'golden age'. When *Hamlet* was written Queen Elizabeth was an old woman with no children of her own. The next in line to the throne was James VI of Scotland, king of England's oldest enemy, and son of Mary Queen of Scots, executed on the orders of Queen Elizabeth some years previously. Civil war, an unpopular king, and acts of revenge against the old order were all possibilities, and may have contributed to an atmosphere of corruption and decay in the play.

Uncertainty: of all Shakespeare's plays *Hamlet* is the one in which the most questions are asked and the fewest answered. Hamlet cannot be certain of how his father died, whether his mother knew or not of his father's murder, if the Ghost is telling the truth, or if his friends are indeed on his side. Hamlet is caught in a web of uncertainty, confusion, and misunderstanding; the harder he struggles, the more he becomes entangled.

Deception and political intrigue are common features in the play, but even the masters of it, Claudius and Polonius, find that events run away with them, and all the intrigue and deception they can muster does not save them from death.

Madness is an excellent protection for Hamlet, because the madman is unpredictable, and is avoided by other people. With both Hamlet and Ophelia, madness is seen as a symbol or sign of a mind that has been pushed beyond the level of tolerance, and which can no longer cope.

Appearance and reality is a major theme in *Hamlet*. Is the Ghost what he appears to be, the spirit of Hamlet's murdered father, or is he a spirit of evil sent to lure Hamlet to his destruction? Is Ophelia in love with Hamlet, or prepared to act merely as Polonius's spy on her ex-lover? Did Gertrude know about the murder of old Hamlet? Is Polonius an old fool, or one of the most dangerous men in the play? Nothing in *Hamlet* is what it seems to be; almost everything could be interpreted in several different ways.

Major issues in *Hamlet*

1. *Hamlet: adolescence and innocence*

One theory which attempts to explain the fascination of the play to successive generations states that the play dramatises the terrible realisation that all young people go through that life is not as simple, as good, or as straightforward as it appeared to be when they were children – a loss of innocence that is both painful and inevitable given a corrupt world and corrupt humanity. The play thus appeals to young people because Hamlet rebels against a cruel world, and to older people he emerges from the painful learning process a better and wiser man.

Hamlet has every possible advantage. He is intelligent, physically proficient, and born into the highest family in the kingdom. He has a loving father and mother, and every advantage that money, rank, and privilege can bring. In a short space of time, one by one, everything that he has relied on in his life is taken away from him, often with cruel force. His father dies, and Hamlet then finds out that he has been murdered by his uncle, who now reigns with every sign of success, thus throwing doubt on family love and the whole honesty of the Danish court, as well as revealing how ruthless the streak of ambition can be in human nature. His mother shames him and the family name by a hasty remarriage, taking away Hamlet's faith in his mother. The girl he appears to have been in love with is caught out acting as a spy on Hamlet for her father and the murdering Claudius. His friends from the University turn out to be acting on the orders of Claudius. Almost at a stroke Hamlet has lost father, mother, lover, and friends, and has been exposed to an ever-widening vein of corruption. It is as if Hamlet, up to the point where the play starts, has been leading his life behind screens which shielded him from the true horror and cruelty and corruption of human life. In a matter of weeks events serve to smash these screens and show him the full corruption and stink of human misdemeanour. In desperation he retreats into an act of madness, in a desperate attempt to gain time to distinguish appearance from reality, truth from deceit. In doing this Hamlet can be seen as the archetypcal adolescent, the young man who has the scales ripped from his eyes, and who suddenly sees life as it really is for the first time, but cannot find the means to confront it. (Before taking this view to heart it might be prudent to remember that *one* view of a play need not be the *only* view of it. It would be quite possible for this idea above to be present in *Hamlet* alongside a number of other themes. Furthermore, why should it only be adolescents who are suddenly forced to lose their innocence and face up to the world as it really is? It would be hard to explain the success achieved by so many relatively old actors – at least in their mid-thirties – if the play were only concerned with adolescence.)

2. *Hamlet: Renaissance man*

Hamlet is sometimes seen as a symbol of the Renaissance man, and the play as a symbol of the impact of the Renaissance on European culture.

When the Roman Empire collapsed Western Europe entered a stage of barbarism and social regression. From the eleventh to the fifteenth centuries Europe began to claw its way back to civilisation, but for all that time achieved nothing nearly so grand and developed as Roman civilisation at its best. During this period, known as the Middle Ages, it was generally held that classical civilisation had seen the ultimate human development, and that succeeding ages could hope at best to emulate that previous development, but never improve on it.

Renaissance means 'rebirth' – the rebirth of learning. It applies to the time, roughly in the sixteenth century, when it was slowly realised that there was new knowledge to be acquired, that the ancient authorities had not always known all there was to know, and that it was possible for humanity to advance anew. Thus Galileo (1564–1642) found proof, as a result of observation – especially with the newly invented telescope – and geometry, that the world was round, and that it revolved around the sun, whereas classical learning had speculated that the earth was flat, and that the sun revolved around it. Galileo was persecuted for maintaining his theories, but the tide was in favour of the new learning.

The Renaissance was a mixed blessing in terms of its impact on society and human thought. It freed humanity of many artificial barriers to learning and the advancement of knowledge, and it made possible modern scientific development. It allowed people to think, explore, experiment, and question, and come to fresh conclusions. In all this it was positive, and hugely exciting. However, there was another side. Human beings had lived with the belief that the world was flat – and with a great many other beliefs – for hundreds and even thousands of years. The old, pre-Renaissance pattern of thought may not have been exciting, but it was safe, and secure. When people start to think, the conclusions they reach cannot be guaranteed to be comfortable or secure. Plunge off into the unknown and anything might happen: thought brings danger, risks, and insecurity, as well as rewards. People who have spent all their lives believing in the old learning, and suddenly find that all they have believed in is a lie, might well react adversely to the shock, like a man who has spent all his life in prison and is suddenly released and told to make his way in the outside world.

In this respect Hamlet can be seen as a symbol of Renaissance man. On the one hand the play is full of the tremendous sense of the potential, beauty, and wonder of man. On the other hand there is a sense of vast fear and despair, because, like Renaissance man, Hamlet has been forsaken by everything on which he used to rely, and has to start anew in everything he thinks and does. This is the risk implicit in the Renaisance – the old barriers are thrown down, but they could stop people from hurting themselves, as well as impeding their advance. This view does point out a basic truth about the play, which is Hamlet's sudden realisation that he lives in a world the complexities of which he has never realised before; but remember that a critic's job is to understand *Hamlet* and a theory involving a complex historical analogy may only be partially helpful in this understanding.

3. *Hamlet and revenge*

Revenge became a very popular theme for plays in Shakespeare's time, so much so that there is a whole 'school' of plays known as 'revenge drama'. Revenge is violent, and exciting; it poses a central moral dilemma which a dramatist of any era can explore. Revenge is forbidden by God in the Old Testament – 'Vengeance is mine, saith the Lord' – and so anyone who exacts personal revenge will be committing a sin for which he can expect damnation. Yet human desire to avenge oneself is immensely strong, and the revenger has to weigh personal desire for revenge against a divine ban on the taking of such revenge.

Revenge confronts Hamlet with a serious problem in the light of this. The Jacobean age saw two types of revenger; the *scourge* who was a man himself evil, damned by God, and chosen by God to destroy others before being destroyed himself; and the *minister*, an inherently good man allowed by God to expose evil without himself becoming contaminated by it. If Hamlet is a scourge, already condemned by God, he might as well kill Claudius immediately and have done with it: he is already condemned by God, and so has nothing to lose by the act of murder. If Hamlet is a minister he must wait for God to give him an opportunity of exposing Claudius. If Hamlet acts immediately to kill Claudius, he loses his immortal soul; if he waits, Claudius might destroy him before he can avenge his father's death. A further complication is the nature of the Ghost. Is he the spirit of Hamlet's father, sent to expose evil, or an evil spirit (in Elizabethan demonology evil spirits could take whatever shape or form they wished) sent to mislead and destroy Hamlet and win his soul for Satan?

Basic questions in *Hamlet*

1. *Why does Hamlet delay?*

Hamlet has every reason to act swiftly in avenging his father; we know he can act quickly, as his behaviour on the pirate ship shows. Yet he seems to find it impossible to kill Claudius, and when he does so it is as an immediate response to the death of his mother. Possible reasons for this delay are:

(*a*) *The earlier play*: there is a theory – but it is no more than a theory – that *Hamlet* is based on another, earlier play with essentially the same story, but which treated the issues raised more simply – for example, Hamlet simply wants revenge, is prevented from enacting it by practical difficulties of killing a reigning king and adopts madness as a ruse to avoid suspicion. This theory coincides with known practice: Shakespeare's age did not prize originality of plot a great deal and the majority of Shakespeare's plays are taken from other books or works. The idea also helps to explain some of the apparent inconsistencies and uncertainties of the play.

In this way, the delay may perhaps be explained by the content of the original version: for example, the practical difficulty of assassinating a monarch surrounded by guards. Perhaps Shakespeare inherited the necessity for delay in the plot, but omitted to expand on its cause.

(*b*) *Intelligence*: perhaps Hamlet is too intelligent: he thinks so much that he thinks himself out of killing Claudius, and substitutes thought for action.

(*c*) *Oedipus*: all children have a natural envy and jealousy of their father because he is a rival for the affection of their mother. Claudius has done what Hamlet would like to do: become the focus of Gertrude's attentions – and so Hamlet cannot kill him because to do so would be to admit to an impulse with which he could not come to terms. A boy's possessive love for his mother is known by psychoanalysts as the 'Oedipus complex' after the character in Greek mythology who unwittingly killed his father, king of Thebes, and became married to his mother.

(*d*) *Shock*: so much has happened to Hamlet in so short a time that he is in a state of shock, and needs time to recover before he can act. Also, murder is a terrifying act, and there is bound to be a totally natural reluctance on the part of a good man to do it.

(*e*) *Uncertainty*: there may be nothing at all odd about the delay: Hamlet has to find out if the Ghost is telling the truth, find an opportunity to kill Claudius, and must wait to see if he is destined to be a 'scourge' or a 'minister'; the delay may therefore be seen as the result of intelligent prudence.

2. Hamlet: 'sweet prince' or 'arrant knave'?

Hamlet subjects Ophelia to mental torture, and possibly drives her to her death. He murders Polonius, who is innocent, and is callous about the murder afterwards. He arranges for his old friends, Rosencrantz and Guildenstern, to be murdered. He places the players in extreme danger. He gives a repulsive reason for not killing Claudius at prayer. He shames Ophelia and himself by his behaviour in her grave. He therefore might well appear as a murdering 'arrant knave'.

On the other hand he is described as a 'sweet prince', and as someone who would have made a good king. He is popular with the people. He is a scholar and a fighter, the best Denmark has. He is a loving and loyal son, and does nothing to bring about the events that lead to the action of the play. He is placed in an appalling predicament and suffers vastly. As far as he is aware Ophelia and Rosencrantz and Guildenstern are spies for Claudius, and have betrayed him. He can and does do evil things; it need not spoil him completely or even partially as a hero, merely make him more realistic. His treatment of Ophelia may be a result of his attitude to women in general, which in turn springs from his reaction to his mother's betrayal of the family honour by her re-marriage.

3. Is Hamlet mad?

Madness symbolises the breakdown of natural order in the mind, a breakdown which in turn reflects the breakdown of all law and natural order in Denmark, where a murderer reigns. Ironically it is the mad people who often speak the truth; this sanity-in-madness is a symbol of a topsy-turvy world where nothing is as expected.

It is however perhaps surprising that there is any question about Hamlet's sanity. Hamlet clearly announces to Horatio that he will feign madness. It allows Hamlet to say things that a sane man would not be permitted to say, and it distances him from other people, who, if they could get closer, might be able to distinguish his real motives. As Hamlet has been under severe strain it is also relatively easy for him to act mad.

The problem is that at times he does it too well, and can give the impression of being truly mad – that is, having lost all rational control over his actions. Only the reader or audience can decide.

Observations and conclusions

The play scene

This is worth close attention as it says a great deal about the theme of appearance and reality. A piece of pure fiction, deliberately made even more unreal by the use of artificial and heightened verse forms, is used to discover a piece of pure fact: Claudius's murder of old Hamlet. Hamlet's instructions to the players are also the closest we come to hearing Shakespeare speak about the rules of acting.

Comedy
Do not overlook the comic element in the play. Hamlet is frequently very witty and funny, and there is a body of opinion which sees all revenge tragedy as being more 'black comedy' (inciting an audience to laughter about events which are serious or revolting) than pure tragedy.

After your reading of *Hamlet* you might like to ask if its only firm conclusion is that humans must suffer what is dealt out to them by Fate with dignity, strength, and without complaint; that humans can never hope to understand the complexity of life. Ask yourself also the significance of Rosencrantz and Guildenstern, Fortinbras, the episode on the pirate ship, why Hamlet leaps into Ophelia's grave when he appears to have regained his sanity, and whether or not Gertrude realises Claudius's guilt.

Macbeth

General points

Macbeth was probably written around 1606. It seems to have been written specifically for the king, James I. James was an expert on witchcraft, and had written a book on the subject. The references to Banquo (an ancestor of James I) founding a line of kings seem to be pure flattery aimed at James. The divine right of kings features heavily in the play and was a favourite topic of James's; there is even mention in the play of 'touching for the king's evil' (whereby the monarch was supposed to be able to cure scrofula), which was something James practised. But although these elements may be there to please James, they all justify their presence in the play for reasons unconnected with patronage.

Indeed, it is sometimes said that James disliked the play, and was frightened by it.

Superstition: the play has a bad name among actors. It is meant to bring very bad luck to any production if a line from *Macbeth*, or the play's title, is spoken backstage, and so amongst actors it is known as 'the Scottish play'.

The text: it has long been thought by critics that the text of *Macbeth* is a bad one, and does not reflect accurately what Shakespeare originally wrote. The Hecate scenes are thought not to be by Shakespeare, and to have been added to the play at some later stage. The play is very short, and is known for the relentless speed of its action, which suggests scenes may have been left out.

Sources: Shakespeare found the story of Macbeth in the book *Chronicles* *of England, Scotland and Ireland* (1577) by Raphael Holinshed (?*d*.1582). Shakespeare alters the story considerably from Holinshed. He compresses the action into about a year, whereas in history Macbeth ruled for nearer twenty years. He makes Duncan old and saintly, whereas in Holinshed he was young and feeble; he gives Macbeth a less good claim to the throne, presents Banquo – in reality an accomplice in Duncan's murder – as a good man, and in general takes every opportunity to blacken Macbeth's character.

Major issues in *Macbeth*

1. *The witches*

The presence of the supernatural in the play is exciting and thrilling. The witches are a physical symbol of the evil which is one of the play's main themes, and they serve to set the atmosphere of the play right from the start, showing that the evil in the play will be of a terrible sort. They give a moral lesson into what happens when people tamper with the Devil or allow themselves to come near him, and they give added insight into both the character of Macbeth and the nature of evil. They tell him no lies, but merely allow him to deceive himself – external evil taking advantage of internal weakness, and blinding Macbeth to the truth. Finally, they are unnatural in the most obvious, physical sense, being neither male nor female, and therefore they symbolise how diseased the universe is in *Macbeth*, and how unnatural are the actions that will take place in the play.

2. *Good versus evil*

The major theme of *Macbeth* is almost the oldest one in history, the battle between good and evil, although the main emphasis in the play is on evil.

It has been suggested that Macbeth and Lady Macbeth are an allegorical portrait of Adam and Eve enacting the Fall of man. The play could be a direct allegory – or is it simply that any play which looks at the fall from grace of a man and his wife who are tempted by the devil will have links with the story of Adam and Eve?

3. *Evil*

Macbeth examines evil in almost its every aspect. In the play it is both an outside, objective force (the witches) and something which is found inside a person, as in Macbeth and Lady Macbeth. Given access, evil can flourish and grow inside a person's mind, but the person concerned must want to do evil before it can affect him.

Evil is seen as an illness; it infects a person, and the infection can be transmitted. The evil in *Macbeth* grows outward to affect everything in Scotland. Ambition is the weakness that lets evil into Macbeth and Lady

Macbeth, and hence into Scotland. A person cannot be evil unless they take a decision to be so, but all people can be affected by evil, whether or not they are evil themselves. This is the horror of evil in *Macbeth*: once it is let loose in society it hurts the innocent and the guilty alike (as is shown by the murder of Lady Macduff and her children). Goodness does not guarantee survival in a society in which evil has been unleashed. Disorder is the symbol of evil, the upsetting of the natural harmony that should exist between human beings, God, and Nature: anything which seeks to destroy the natural order (and the murder of a king is such an act because it seeks to replace the king chosen by God with one chosen by a man) is therefore by definition evil.

When evil has destroyed all that it can, it then turns on and destroys itself, killing its bearers. Unfortunately this self-destruction can only take place at a vast cost in suffering and death.

4. *Ambition and regicide*

Ambition and regicide (the murder of a king) are two types of evil examined very closely in *Macbeth*. Ambition is seen as a sin, an attempt to jump the natural order and make a new one, a desire so intense it can lead a person into the hands of evil. Regicide is to kill God's annointed king, and so likewise to disrupt the natural and divine order. Macbeth's illegal and immoral kingship brings death, destruction, and suffering to Scotland, whilst the good kingship of Duncan and Malcolm brings victory and happiness; the contrast is deliberate.

5. *Appearance and reality*

Murdering Duncan appears to be the right thing for Macbeth to do; the witches appear to be predicting success for him; kingship appears to be all a man and woman could ask for in life – but in each case the appearance is wrong, and the reality is that evil is attempting to drag Macbeth to his destruction. Duncan himself says ironically that one cannot tell a person's character from his face, not realising that Macbeth is about to betray and kill him. As in *Hamlet*, things are not what they might seem to be on the surface, and the ability to distinguish appearance from reality is crucial.

Basic questions in *Macbeth*

1. *'This dead butcher and his fiend-like queen'?*

Is Macbeth merely a 'butcher' and Lady Macbeth a 'fiend' or devil?

Macbeth murders Duncan with his own hands. He murders Banquo and tries to murder Fleance, and wipes out the family of Macduff. All his victims are innocent of any crime, and in murdering his king Macbeth is guilty of one of the greatest crimes possible. Macbeth associates with witches and the powers of evil, and unleashes a reign of terror in

Scotland. Lady Macbeth is instrumental in persuading Macbeth to murder Duncan, is ruthlessly ambitious, and is prepared to sacrifice her fertility and femininity to the powers of evil. She commits suicide at the end of the play, an act seen as a sin by the Church.

On the other hand Macbeth has been a noble servant of Scotland, is a brave and very capable soldier, and is responsible for beating rebels who threaten the security of the kingdom. After the murder of Duncan, the murder of Banquo is an act of self-defence, and there is every sign that Macbeth might might have been a good king under normal circumstances. The witches and Lady Macbeth are partly responsible for his murder of Duncan. A butcher might not be expected to undergo the suffering that Macbeth clearly undergoes, and a fiend would hardly suffer so much as to make her want to commit suicide.

Part of the answer to this question is that Macbeth and Lady Macbeth either are or become evil, but that Shakespeare still manages to retain a degree of sympathy from the audience – for Macbeth in particular. It is done by including many testimonies to the previous skill, bravery, and courage of Macbeth from other characters: by his wife saying that he is 'full of the milk of human kindness'; by having some of the blame for his act of murder shifted on to Lady Macbeth and the witches; by the fact that his great sin is ambition, one for which most people can feel some sympathy; by his own uncertainty before and after the murder, showing that he has feelings and a degree of humanity; by his suffering, and his ability to express that suffering, which automatically attracts a measure of sympathy; and by the fact that the audience never actually sees Macbeth commit any of his murders – all they see is the suffering they bring him. The fact that he dies fighting, even though he knows that he has lost everything, also adds to his stature and the respect he can command.

2. Whose fault is it?

Macbeth murders Duncan, but it is possible to place some of the blame for this on firstly the witches, who lure him on by attractive-sounding prophecies and treat his acquisition of the kingship as if it were a foregone conclusion; and secondly on his wife, who abuses him when he wishes to pull out of the murder plot, and persuades him to carry out the murder. Yet in the final count it is his decision, his responsibility, and his hands which actually plunge the dagger into Duncan.

Observations and conclusions

Characters

Macbeth and Lady Macbeth are the only fully-developed characters in the play. At the start of the play Lady Macbeth is stronger in will than Macbeth; as the play progresses they exchange roles, with Macbeth becoming the dominant partner and Lady Macbeth declining and finally collapsing into suicide.

Imagery

The *imagery* in Macbeth is remarkably concentrated. Blood, darkness, and the colour red are heavily emphasised and frequently mentioned, as is polluted, foul, or dirty air. Violent imagery of tumult, storm, and physical injury is also common. Lack of sleep is associated with guilt and evil; babies and children are associated with the natural order. Macbeth's destruction or attempted destruction of two families (those of Banquo and Macduff) takes on added significance when it is seen that the family is the symbol of a healthy and fertile society.

The image of loose or ill-fitting clothing is a unique feature of *Macbeth*; it makes Macbeth laughable, and also shows that his achievements never quite come to fit him, and that he can never be at ease with what he has obtained.

Othello

General points

Othello is sometimes referred to as a 'domestic tragedy'. In *Hamlet*, *Macbeth*, and *King Lear* the fate of whole nations is at stake; in *Othello* the loss of Venice's best general is a major inconvenience, but it hardly compares with the death of whole royal families. Furthermore, the gods, Destiny, and Fate play little apparent part in *Othello*. It is one man – Iago – who largely destroys Othello, and the play lacks the supernatural element found in the other three great tragedies. Even its characters are of much lower rank than in the other three plays – the highest ranking figure is the Duke of Venice, and there are no kings, emperors, or even princes in the play. The fact that *Othello* differs in these ways from the other plays does not make it any less of a great play; it merely makes it somewhat different.

Regeneration: the play has also been criticised for being just a 'parade of pain', and a tragedy without meaning, implying that all the play consists of is the murder of a totally innocent woman and the utter degradation and destruction of a good man (Othello) by a bad man (Iago). According to this view the play ends with little or no feeling of regeneration, or awareness of a society purged of its evil, and is merely a horror story dressed up with poetry. The other side would argue that the feelings aroused by the suffering and death of Othello are magnificently tragic in the fullest sense of the word, and that his realisation of his mistakes and his acquisition of self-knowledge at the end of the play mean that he dies with the utmost dignity and a sense of tragic waste.

Major issues in *Othello*

1. *Jealousy*

It is often said that *Othello* is about jealousy and its ability to destroy a man and all that he loves. Othello is made jealous of Desdemona by Iago, and Iago is himself jealous of Cassio, and possibly of Othello. Iago, the jealous villain, succeeds in infecting Othello, someone who is 'not easily jealous', with jealousy, and thus draws him down to his own level.

2. *Appearance and reality*

As is so often the case in Shakespeare's plays, Othello's fall comes about partly because he cannot distinguish appearance from reality, what is real from what is false. He cannot see that Iago is evil, and that the goodness of Desdemona is real, any more than Macbeth can see the real nature of the witches, or King Lear the real nature of Goneril and Regan.

There are two lessons implicit in the appearance and reality theme in the play: the inability to distinguish truth from deceit is a recipe for disaster; evil is very rarely honest about its own nature, and always seeks to disguise itself.

3. *Misunderstanding*

Othello can also be seen as a tragedy of misunderstanding. If Othello understood Desdemona he would not doubt her, and if he understood Iago he would not trust him. If Desdemona understood Othello properly she would know that his love for her went so deep that any threat to it would induce destruction of them both. If Emilia understood the true depth of evil in Iago she would not give him the handkerchief, and tragedy would be averted.

A major misunderstanding is that of Iago. He is a cynic, and a coarse, crude man. Love to him is animal coupling, and he cannot understand the nature of true love, because he is not capable of giving or receiving it himself. As a result he does not understand and chronically underestimates the power of love, the power that is summoned by his plotting and which eventually destroys him as well as Othello and Desdemona.

4. *Reason versus instinct*

The play can be seen as a battle between reason and instinct. When Othello acts on instinct he is usually right; when he tries to reason or think things out, he is usually wrong. Perhaps this does not merit the grand title of a theme, but is simply an aspect of Othello's character. He is not the most intellectually gifted of Shakespeare's tragic heroes: his passionate nature can cloud his reason and prevent him from having a clear understanding of his circumstances.

5. *Isolation*

Again, isolation may not be a theme, but it is certainly a strong consideration in the play. Othello is a very isolated figure. He is isolated by his colour, which makes him almost unique in Venice, and his race, which means he was not born into the ways of Venice. He has lived all his life as a soldier, and so his lack of knowledge of how the world works further isolates him from those he meets. This isolation leaves him more open than would otherwise be the case to the words of Iago – one of the few people he feels he can trust and who breaches his isolation – and more willing to believe that a Venetian lady would behave as he is told Desdemona has.

6. *Honour*

Honour is another strong presence in the play, visible on three levels:

(*a*) *Marital honour*: Othello believes that his wife's unfaithfulness is a reflection and a tarnishing of his own honour, which can only be cleansed by killing her and her lover.

(*b*) *Parental honour*: Brabantio feels that his honour as a parent has been damaged and reduced by his daughter's elopement.

(*c*) *Professional honour*: Cassio feels he has lost the immortal part of himself, his honour as a soldier, when he shames himself while drunk. Iago's loss of honour when Cassio is promoted instead of him may well be a strong influence on his feelings towards Othello.

7. *Love*

It is as well not to lose sight of the fact that *Othello* also has *love* and *evil* as two of its main themes; it is in effect the story of an affair of love that is blighted by evil influence and has its raw power turned in on itself with hugely destructive effects.

Major questions in *Othello*

1. *Othello: noble moor or hollow egotist?*

One view of Othello sees him as a noble moor, a blameless and passionate hero. Another says that Othello's apparent nobility is hollow, and that he is an egotist, someone who does not know either himself or his wife, who tries to make excuses at the end of the play for what he has done, and who never really admits his guilt. By this account Othello has a tremendous capacity for seeing what he wants to see, and believing what he wants to believe.

Othello can speak marvellous poetry, and at times in the play shows himself to be noble, magnanimous, exotic, regal – and egotistical. He is a magnificent soldier. He never ceases to love Desdemona, even during and after killing her. He is widely admired and loved by other characters, and even Iago admits his essential goodness. He is proud of what he has achieved, but it is proper pride, no more than his due. He accepts at the end of the play that he must be punished or punish himself for what he has done. He is destroyed by the power of his love, but the fact that he can love at so high a rate and so great a strength is a point in his favour.

On the debit side, he allows himself to be fooled by Iago. He lacks finesse or subtlety in his responses. He is a relatively simple soul, and his intellect is easily confused; it is always a risk in the play that he appears stupid in not seeing through Iago and realising the truth. He is not naturally jealous, but when incited to jealousy it takes complete control of him. He behaves despicably to Desdemona, first striking her and then killing her. He overstates things, and possibly dramatises them too much. He is strong-willed, but is this nobility of passion or simple stubborness?

Othello is very trusting. This may be his downfall, but it is a feature shared by many of Shakespeare's noblest characters. He has hardly had time to get to know Desdemona, and Iago is a tried and trusted colleague in arms. He is a man of action, and is easily confused when faced with a wide range of options, but this again is merely normal. Perhaps it is simply that Othello has too much passion, which Iago turns to hatred. Perhaps the tragedy is that a great and noble man under normal circumstances could have lived at total peace with the world and his wife, but a tragic turn of events condemns him and Desdemona for faults that otherwise might never have surfaced.

2. *Iago: motiveless malignancy or hurt pride?*

As with Othello, there are two distinct views of Iago. One view sees him as acting without true motive. He is possessed by evil without understanding why this is so, loves evil for its own sake, and is a born destroyer who works by destructive instinct and not rational thought. The other view states that Iago has ample motives for what he does. He is jealous of Cassio, thinks he has been cuckolded by Othello and Cassio, and lusts after Desdemona, as well as being jealous of her place in Othello's affections. This view sees Iago as an opportunist, with no far-sighted plan. He wishes to cause as much suffering as possible to Othello, but is taken by surprise with the force of passion he arouses in him, and is forced to try for Desdemona's death when it becomes clear that he has driven Othello too far, and Desdemona must be killed if he, Iago, is to survive.

Whichever view you take, bear in mind the theory that Iago has 'bull-ring fever', a form of blood lust. He becomes addicted to the excitement and risk of plotting, so he cannot stop it even when it threatens his own destruction.

Observations and conclusions

Iago

Iago has to be convincing in his duplicity. If he shows his evil too clearly Othello can then very easily appear simply a fool for believing, and if this happens it might well be difficult for an audience to accept Othello as a tragic hero worthy of its pity and respect.

Desdemona

One of the purest good characters in Shakespeare: Brabantio stresses her innocence; Roderigo falls in love with her; Iago admires her; Cassio overflows with chaste admiration of her; the worldly-wise and cynical Emilia is prepared to die for her; and she tries to protect Othello even after he has all but killed her. At no time is she unfaithful or disloyal to Othello, whatever the provocation. On the other hand, she misjudges the strength of Othello's feeling about Cassio, and lies about the handkerchief, a major factor in bringing about her own destruction, but this is a fault of judgment rather than a display of any evil. She could be criticised only for playing too passive a role.

Imagery

The imagery reflects the characterisation. In the first three acts Iago uses a great deal of animal imagery, either predatory animals or simply revolting or disgusting animals. As Iago gains more of a hold over Othello, from Act 3 onwards, so Othello begins to use more and more of this same imagery, illustrating the increasing corruption in Othello's mind. Imagery of the Devil follows the same pattern. There are sixty-four diabolic images in the play, with Iago speaking eighteen and Othello twenty-six: but fourteen of Iago's are in the first two acts, twenty-five of Othello's in the last three. The word 'honest' is heavily used in the play, fifty-two times in all and mostly of Iago. It can mean bluff and forthright, or have its modern meaning, and there is much ironical counterplay between the two meanings.

Othello tends to talk romantically of things, Iago practically. Wealth to Othello is pearls and 'chrysolite', whilst to Iago it is just money. Light and dark imagery starts as a simple contrast between complexions, then takes on moral overtones (the devilish blackness of Othello covering a noble soul), and later is used by Othello to illustrate what he sees as the white purity of Desdemona concealing her black and sin-stained soul.

King Lear

General points

The Tate Version: for over one hundred and fifty years, between 1681 and 1838, the version of *King Lear* performed in England was not that by Shakespeare but an adaptation written by Nahum Tate (1652–1715). This version left out the Fool and France, and created a happy ending: Lear lives, and so does Cordelia, who marries Edgar. Altering texts in this manner has not a great deal to commend it, and the Tate version of the play is a mockery of the real thing. But the fact that it was written in the first place does help to point out firstly how implausible certain parts of the original play are, and secondly how horrific the original ending is. It can be argued that Tate made the events in the play more credible, and simply gave audiences the ending they yearn for.

Justice: several critics have found the ending of the play contrary to 'natural ideas of justice', and have suggested that the deaths of Lear and Cordelia deny all moral laws and values, are wholly unfair, and are examples of needless, random cruelty. In this respect audience response to the play can be similar to the 'howl' that is Lear's response to Cordelia's death.

Improbability: *King Lear* is sometimes cited as one of Shakespeare's most improbable plays. Edgar and Kent continue in disguise long after the apparent purpose of their disguise has been served. Gloucester is willing to believe firstly that Edgar would write to Edmund when they live in the same house, and secondly that he would put down self-damning views on paper. Gloucester apparently cannot recognise his own son's handwriting or his voice, and feels a strange need to go to Dover to commit suicide; he is also blinded when reason dictates he should be killed. Lear's motives for dividing his kingdom can appear tenuous, and Edmund waits far too long to tell people that he has ordered the deaths of Lear and Cordelia, and is out of character anyway in doing it at all.

It is, however, as well to bear in mind that many of these improbabilities are nowhere near as apparent on stage as they are when the play is read, and in any event all plays have their own internal standards of reality which are not always those of the real world.

Comedy: many of the episodes in the play could provoke laughter. The trial scene, Gloucester's failed suicide, Edgar's use of a coarse accent when he fights Oswald, and Lear's madness are all in this category. Perhaps the comedy is intentional, forcing the audience to laugh bitterly at an absurd world and the absurd antics of those who inhabit it;

perhaps it is an error on Shakespeare's part; perhaps it is not comedy at all. Doubts over such issues offer a director the freedom to exploit them according to his own interpretation.

Vastness: many critics have commented on the feeling of vastness in *King Lear*, a huge, wild passion in its writing, and the feeling that the play touches the very heart of existence. One view has it that the play is so vast in its scope and so demanding of its actors that it is essentially impractical for performance.

Major issues in *King Lear*

1. *The Christian/redemptive approach*

This view of the play interprets it in mystical, religious terms. Lear and Gloucester are purged of their spiritual blindness, stripped by suffering and madness of their pomp and 'superfluity', and forced thereby into seeing their real nature, the real nature of others, and the real nature of life. Their original misguided actions allow evil to enter the world, which as always in tragedy brings punishment for them and introduces death and destruction into the rest of society, affecting guilty and innocent alike. The tragic hero must die for his sins, but when he does so death is a release rather than a punishment: Lear has lost the world, but saved his soul. The audience leave the play shaken, shocked, but also reassured, partly because under terrifying pressure the tragic hero has revealed the true nobility and strength of mankind, and partly because by the end of the play evil has been destroyed, society purged, and the world is ready to go back to its normal state. Edgar is left to carry on, and, as someone who has also been purged through a form of madness, he can carry out the lessons and the philosophy learned by Lear and Gloucester. It is sometimes held by those who support this view that Lear dies of unbearable joy at the end of the play, believing Cordelia to be still alive.

2. *The pessimistic/nihilistic view*

This view takes exactly the opposite line from the redemptive view discussed above. According to this line of thought there is no redemption or regeneration in *King Lear*; it is the most appallingly pessimistic of Shakespeare's plays. It states there is no Divinity, Providence, or guiding hand in the world, with man a raging beast and gloom and despondency the key note of the final scene. Lear, Cordelia, and Gloucester are punished far in excess of their crime. The ending of the play is so horrific that it had to be altered for one hundred and fifty years, and Lear is destroyed after he has gained his new-found knowledge, making his death even more meaningless. The word 'nothing' is mentioned numerous times in the play, and emptiness of hope and spirit is all that awaits man. Lear's insight allows him to see the bitter truth of what man is: isolated, alone, and weak – in effect, Poor Tom. Nearly every character appeals to the gods, yet the appeals and the attitudes are contradictory and cancel each other out, the conclusion being that there is no God. Edgar is left to carry on, but the weight of tragedy is so heavy that it allows not the slightest hint of cheerfulness to enliven the gloom at the end of the play. Suffering without redemption is what the play offers, a vision of a lunatic, absurd world.

3. *The collapse of order*

King Lear can be seen as a vision of the end of the world, what happens when the Elizabethan concept of order falls apart and anarchy and chaos are let loose in the world. In Lear's world all values, codes, and order have been turned on their heads. Children betray their fathers, the honest are banished and the guilty rewarded, madmen speak the truth and sane men behave like madmen, people 'see' only when they are blind, family and natural ties of kinship are broken, the king is a beggar, son kills father, sister murders sister, human beings sink lower than animals, and the heavens rage in fury. This viewpoint does not prejudge whether or not order is restored at the end of the play; it merely points out the picture of order being broken.

4. *Values*

There are certain values which emerge from *King Lear* regardless of the conclusions reached about redemption and regeneration.

(*a*) *Love*: All the good characters in the play have a capacity for selfless love and loyalty. Lear and Gloucester gain this quality, Cordelia, Kent, and Edgar have it, and it is even present at the level of the servant who kills Cornwall, and the old man who helps Gloucester. This love leads nowhere and earns no earthly reward, but the mere fact of its existence is hopeful.

There are two divisions of character in the play. Some are governed solely by logic and self interest (Edmund, Goneril, Regan, Cornwall) who renounce love and are motivated solely by self-interest. These are the purely rational people. The other group (Lear and Gloucester) are without rationality, but have an excess of passion. This latter group is preferable to the former, but neither is right – as in *Othello*, the ideal character has an ability to love selflessly, but the capacity to add a degree of thought and reason to this as well.

(*b*) *Patience*: the play seems to value highly patience, endurance, and fortitude. If justice in the world is rash, unpredictable, or even does not exist at all, then patience and the virtues of endurance become even more significant.

Edmund and the Fool can be seen to symbolise two ways of responding to an unjust world: Edmund's response is to manipulate, coldly and cynically, people for selfish ends, the Fool's way to accept everything, and laugh at the unavoidable idiocy of it all.

5. *Justice*
Justice must rank as a major concern of the play. There is the whole question of whether or not Lear in the main plot and Gloucester in the sub-plot receive justice, and whether or not the ending is just. Lear fiercely questions the justice of the world and what has happened to him; there is the mad mock trial scene. The issue may ultimately pass beyond justice and question who governs the world – what is the nature of the gods?

6. *Kingship and office*
Kingship is a central issue in *King Lear*. Lear forgets that the pomp and circumstance, the 'superfluity' has to be earned, and that he cannot hold on to these (symbolised by his hundred knights) and get rid of his duties, as he tries to. Lear forgets also that for all his glamour the king is still a man, a 'poor, bare, forked animal'. He tells himself in the storm to 'take physic, pomp' – in other words, to learn that the king is a man like his subjects. The need to acquire self-knowledge marches alongside the lessons of kingship. Lear 'hath ever but slenderly known himself', and the action of the play forces him to acquire the self-knowledge he should have had in the first place.

Major questions in *King Lear*

1. *Is Lear a man more sinned against than sinning?*
This question relates to the whole issue and theme of justice, and its existence or otherwise in *King Lear*. On the one hand Lear gives in to flattery, makes a bad decision to split his kingdom, and when he does so splits it unfairly. He banishes cruelly the only daughter who loves him, and a nobleman who is devoted to his service. He attempts to live like a king with none of a king's responsibilities or duties, and takes himself out into a storm when his followers are dismissed. On the other hand he is punished for his lack of self-knowledge, his vanity, and his inability to distinguish the truth from falsehood by losing his wealth, his sanity, his daughter, and finally his life. He has certainly sinned, but only through common faults which under different circumstances might have gone unnoticed and unpunished.

2. *Why does Lear go mad?*
Lear goes mad because he is robbed of the honour, respect, and kindness due to a King, a father, and an old man. He cannot avoid the realisation that these are being denied him; he cannot face the realisation that it is partly through his own fault, and the conflict tears his mind apart. Also the denial of family implicit in his treatment suggests a collapse in the

order that binds the universe together. His suffering enforces self-knowledge, with which initially he cannot cope. His suffering and part-knowledge also show him a hitherto unsuspected cruel and harsh world where good and evil alike die and suffer. This new insight (as is the case with Hamlet) induces madness and helps to preserve it in him.

3. *What is the function of the Fool?*

The Fool provides humour in the play by parodying its serious themes. He also shows the audience the truth through his capacity to see things in their bare essentials. He provides a common-sense vision of events in the play. He acts like a Chorus, pointing out what is happening and increasing the pain and the pathos by his humour. He alone realises fully the incongruities that typify the play – the king reduced to a beggar, the Fool the only wise man in the court, and so forth. When Lear attains a similar degree of knowledge and insight in and after his madness, the Fool is seen no more: he is no longer necessary, because Lear has taken his place.

4. *How effective is the portrait of Cordelia?*

Cordelia is the only daughter who loves her father truly. She is banished unfairly, but returns to save him when he is in need and when she could easily have left him. She cherishes and loves him to the utmost. As such she appears to offer a portrait of complete goodness. One drawback to her portrayal is that, of necessity, she vanishes off the scene for quite a while, during which time the audience may lose interest in her.

It is sometimes asked why she does not flatter her father. This would cost her little, as she does love him a great deal, and it would please an old man. By being so brutally honest and refusing to change her mind she brings about no positive result, and in fact helps to ensure the destruction of her father by giving the kingdom to Goneril and Regan. She has been described as a bore, and as stubborn as her father.

Observations and conclusions

Sub-Plot

King Lear has one of the best-developed sub-plots of any play by Shakespeare. The aim of any sub-plot is to provide variety and relief, and to highlight the themes and action of the main plot by looking at them from a different angle. Main plot and sub-plot have to be separate, but also linked if the audience are not to be presented with the confusing spectacle of two separate plays masquerading as one. In *King Lear* both plots feature old men who misjudge their children and so invite disaster through their 'blindness'. Both undergo appalling suffering, both are saved by the children they rejected, and both die. Edmund is a major link between the two plots. The characters in the sub-plot moralise much more than those in the main plot, and the sub-plot is more improbable than the main plot. In general the sub-plot looks rather more simply and straightforwardly at the issues raised in the main plot.

Madness
Madness comes into all the tragedies in one form or another – at least if Othello is deemed to be mad at the height of his anguish. Madness in *King Lear* is a response to intolerable mental pressure, a purging process which strips the mind of layer upon layer of deceit and hypocrisy and cleanses and purifies it through pain. Edgar is a lesser man than Lear, but he too must go through a form of madness (albeit a lesser one) if he is to acquire the knowledge needed to take over from Lear. Edgar's 'Poor Tom' is a picture of basic man, the primitive animal which will always exist whatever clothes and finery 'civilised' man adopts.

Henry IV Part 1 and *Henry IV Part 2*

General points

The section on the history plays in Part 2 of this Handbook (pages 40–3) outlines the general development of the 'second tetralogy' of Shakespeare's plays, and the thematic links between the four plays in the tetralogy. In brief, Richard II is shown as a man with the right to rule, but not the skill or temperament; Henry IV as a man with the skill to rule, but as a usurper and the murderer of the previous king he does not have the right to rule. Finally Henry V inherits the crown properly from his father, and therefore has a right to rule, and also has the skill that Richard II lacked; he is therefore shown as the ideal king.

Kingship: Shakespeare's history plays are based around the belief that only God can 'make' a king, which He does through the hereditary principle. If God chooses to make someone king who is not good at the job, then this can be seen as Divine punishment; in any case there is nothing that any human being is permitted to do about it. Man is not only forbidden to make anyone king; he is also forbidden to remove someone appointed by God from the throne. The punishment for usurpation (removing a king from his throne) is a troubled reign, a rebellious nation, and often death and destruction.

Two plays: Prince Hal appears to reform twice in *Henry IV Part 1* and *Henry IV Part 2*, once in each play. This and other oddities in the two plays has led some critics to believe that Shakespeare originally planned to write only the one play, but then found himself with too much material and round about Act 3 in *Henry IV Part 1* decided to write two plays and not one. Another view is that *Henry IV Part 2* was written simply to capitalise on the success of *Henry IV Part 1*, rather in the same way that a modern film which is a success will soon have a sequel written, often bearing the same name.

The change in the plays: most critics would agree that there is a distinct darkening of the tone in *Henry IV Part 2*, and that *Henry IV Part 1* is lighter and more comic. If this is true, it may be a result of Shakespeare attempting to show that the problems of rebellion and disorder are serious enough to warrant the rejection of Falstaff, as well as a reflection of the growing seriousness of England's unhealthy state.

Plot and sub-plot: both plays have a well-defined plot and sub-plot. The main plot centres on the court of England, rebellion, and Henry IV, whilst the sub-plot centres on Falstaff and the Boar's Head Tavern. The sub-plot is therefore primarily comic, but still throws a great deal of light on the concerns of the main plot. Prince Hal is the major figure linking the two plots.

Major issues in *Henry IV Part 1* and *Henry IV Part 2*

---

1. *Honour*

A distinct theme in *Henry IV Part 1* is that of honour, and at the outset of the play this theme is summed up and represented by the figure of Hotspur. Hotspur represents chivalric honour, the honour of the fighting man, as formulated by medieval tradition. As the play proceeds the faults in this theory of honour are clearly shown. Shakespeare never denies the necessity or the honourable nature of military skill and chivalry – after all, the symbol of Hal's acquisition of honour is his defeat of Hotspur in a fair fight – but he does show that it is not enough to ensure survival or the correct fulfilment of a kingly role. Hotspur is portrayed as a limited character. He may have all the military and chivalric honour there is, but he is a quick-tempered, rash, and politically naïve man whose short-sightedness allows him to be a party to a proposed division of the kingdom.

Hotspur's brand of honour is shown as lacking in many respects what, for example, a good king would need to see him through a successful reign. In the final count, Hotspur's honour is too tied to selfish glory, too personal to be right for the king who has to act on behalf of his country rather than himself. However, it is possible to see considerable sadness in Shakespeare's dismissal of Hotspur's brand of honour, with all its glory and simplicity, inevitable though its decline might be. Perhaps Shakespeare accepts the need for something more complex, whilst at the same time regretting the passing of the old order.

Hal gains martial honour in *Henry IV Part 1* by his defeat of Hotspur and by his offer to face Hotspur in single combat. Some critics see it as a weakness of the two plays that Hal then appears to relapse, go back to his old haunts and Falstaff, and has to prove himself a second time to his father in *Henry IV Part 2*.

2. *Disorder*

England is seen as sick and diseased, and this impression increases as the two plays advance. Prime symbols of disorder are the illness of Henry IV himself, and the continual rebellions faced by Henry. It is Henry's usurpation of the crown that has brought this sickness to the state, and its effect is to impose cruel disorder on the nation.

Disorder is seen in Falstaff and all he does. He is the force of vice that can wipe out law and order, and which operates only on rampant sensuality and self-interest. The fact that this can be attractive only adds to its threat. The harsh reality of disorder is seen in Gloucestershire first when Falstaff corruptly recruits soldiers, and secondly when his response to the news that Hal is king is that he now controls the laws of England. Equally, the symbol of Hal's willingness and ability to clean England of its corruption is his decision to champion his and Falstaff's old enemy, the Lord Chief Justice, and to reject Falstaff.

3. *The rejection of Falstaff*

The rejection of Falstaff provides what is almost certainly the major issue of the two plays. It is presaged in *Henry IV Part 1* when in what starts as play-acting in the Boar's Head suddenly turns into a serious expression of views, with Hal promising to reject Falstaff; this occurs as planned at the end of *Henry IV Part 2*. The problem lies in deciding whether or not the audience feel their sympthy lies with Falstaff, rather than with Hal; perhaps Shakespeare actually intended this to express the view that the price paid for Hal's kingship is as high as the sacrifice required of him to reject Falstaff.

Falstaff is one of the most famous comic characters ever created. Despite his undoubted evil, he is attractive. His crimes are rarely committed on stage, and those that are are relatively minor. He has a hugely infectious gaiety and zest for life, and this, together with his refusal to take anything seriously, makes him admirable. The audience gain vast enjoyment from his ability to extricate himself from any scrape. Falstaff is also completely honest about his evil, never seriously trying to hide it except in boasting that is so untrue as to be clearly a fable. Thus the audience feel that anyone taken in by his evil must be so blind as to the real nature of things as to deserve all they get. Falstaff's evil is never a threat to the audience, because to them he is never hypocritical. He does, furthermore, appear to have some real affection for the Prince, and, coward though he may be, he does actually stay to exchange a few blows with his adversaries at Gad's Hill, escapes from an encounter with the feared Douglas at Shrewsbury, and is brave enough to go into battle with a bottle of drink in his holster instead of a pistol. His rejection can therefore be seen as cruel and callous, a sign that laughter and fun are not possible in the new order that Hal will usher in.

On the other hand, Hal has a straight choice between riot, vice, and anarchy in Falstaff, and law and order in the Lord Chief Justice, and to choose the former would be to deny his willingness to rule for the greater good of England. Falstaff appears to be based partly on the old Vice figure of the morality plays, and as such the Elizabethan audience would have been expecting Vice to be disposed of at the end of the play. The audience are warned far in advance that Falstaff will be rejected, as is Falstaff, and only Falstaff's ability to deceive himself preserves him from the truth of what will happen. Hal and Falstaff are rarely in each other's company in *Henry IV Part 2*, which may lessen the shock of rejection, and the Falstaff of *Henry IV Part 2* is a much more seedy and threatening figure than his predecessor in *Henry IV Part 1*. He is now shown as sick and diseased, and more prone to worry about death. His dealings with Mistress Quickly are shabby, and his instruction to Bardolph, 'Hook on, hook on', suggests he is a predator rather than a jolly companion. His associates are deliberately blackened towards the end of the play, and the sheer power of Falstaff's greed is emphasised in the Justice Shallow scenes, themselves a symbol of how far corruption and decay have advanced in England. Finally, in his rejection Hal appears to be on the edge of joking again at Falstaff; he then merely banishes him, and provides a pension for him. It can be argued that Hal banishes Falstaff out of a human desire to protect the fat old knight, and because Hal, far from being a ruthless power-seeker, is frightened that Falstaff will win him round. It is worth bearing in mind that the rejection scene can be played as being as hard for Hal as it is for Falstaff.

There can be little doubt that Hal ought to banish Falstaff if he is to become the perfect king. The question is whether or not in banishing him he makes too great a sacrifice of his humanity for his own character, and the audience, to bear.

4. *Kingship*

The issue of usurpation and the right of kings to rule has been discussed above, but the theme of kingship in the plays also comments at length on the nature of the ideal king, and the sacrifice and strain necessary to become one. The perfect king is religious, lawfully appointed to the throne, courageous and skilful in battle, just, fair, and honest, dignified, efficient, free from personal ambition and sin, and has a knowledge of those he governs (this latter necessity is cited by Hal as one of the reasons for his attendance at the Boar's Head). Both plays also make very clear that kingship involves suffering and sacrifice on the part of the king. In both plays Hal bemoans the fact that he never asked or wished for the kingship, and both he and his father exemplify the price of kingship.

Major questions in *Henry IV Part 1* and *Henry IV Part 2*

Most of the central questions about these two plays have been covered above, but there are two other areas of doubt that should be examined.

1. *Who is the real hero of the plays?*
There are three major characters in both plays: Hal, Falstaff, and Henry IV. This trio of major characters has led some critics to suggest that not one of them can claim to be the hero or even the central figure of the plays, but that the real hero is the country of England. It is true that audience attention is divided amongst three characters (four if Hotspur is included in *Henry IV Part 1*), and that the health and future of England is an overriding concern in both plays. It is also true that the plays make some attempt at being a 'social panorama', an attempt to illustrate and reveal English society from top (the court) to bottom (the Boar's Head).

On the other hand it is also true that more and more attention is focussed on Hal as the plays proceed; he could well be seen as the central figure in the sense that every issue and character in the play comes back to Hal at some time or other, and in the sense that it is kingship and the perfect king that is the play's main concern.

2. *Can we sympathise with the rebels?*
People have felt sympathy for Falstaff; it is also possible to feel sympathy for the rebels, in both plays. Hotspur can be an attractive figure, and he clearly has some cause for complaint against Henry. Only one rebel is shown as totally evil, Worcester, and it can be argued that he is the only villain amongst the rebels, largely because he keeps the truth of Henry's offer before Shrewsbury from Hotspur. Prince John appears to treat the rebels in a dishonourable and shabby way in *Henry IV Part 2*.

It is possible to argue that the audience's sympathy is aroused, mildly, but that this does not preclude their condemnation, just as the audience sympathise with Macbeth but recognise the necessity of his death; or indeed just as they recognise the inevitability of what must happen to Falstaff. It is also possible to argue that the crime of rebellion is shown as so terrible that no sympathy is possible, under any circumstances.

Observations and conclusions

These two plays are possibly the most *political* that Shakespeare ever wrote, in the sense of their being an examination in detail of how kingship and government operate in both the ideal world of theory and the corrupt world of practice. As modern productions have shown, the key to the plays is the portrayal of Falstaff and Hal; the emotional depth of the plays can depend on the extent to which the actor playing Hal can show him as doing the right thing, but only at a price. It is relatively easy for Hal to lose the sympathy of the audience, for the ironical reason that Shakespeare comes near to creating a king who is *too* perfect – and an excess of perfection can breed resentment from an audience possessed of a normal ration of sinfulness.

Twelfth Night

General points

Twelfth Night was written between 1598 and 1600. It is often held to be the last of the 'happy' comedies, and Shakespeare was soon to write *Hamlet* and the great tragedies. *Twelfth Night* is a comedy – it has a happy ending, and no-one is killed in the action – but it also contains a surprising number of references to violence, death, and loss, and hints of a darker and more sombre world occur throughout the play.

Viola: it was obviously tempting for Elizabethan and Jacobean authors to write parts in which the leading female characters dressed up as men, because all female parts were played by boys, and the adoption of a boy acting a female wearing men's clothes allowed the author to engage in considerable irony. There is a suggestion that the play as we have it was altered at some stage. Viola announces that she will go to Orsino's court as a eunuch, which implies she will sing to him, but no further mention of her singing is made; when a song is sung in Orsino's court the credence of the audience can be overstretched by the fact that Feste is sent for to sing it: Viola would be a much more obvious choice for singer. The sudden appearance of Fabian as a character is also odd. He comes as if from nowhere, and takes the part in the orchard scene that one might well imagine Feste playing. One possible – and unprovable – explanation is that the voice of the actor playing Viola broke prior to a performance of the play, and that whilst he was still sufficiently treble to cope with the spoken word, singing was beyond him. Thus the songs had to be transferred to Feste, and Fabian's part written in to take on some of the extra load. (Speculation such as this does no harm, provided it is carefully treated, since it focusses attention on the fact that Shakespeare was writing for the live theatre, where circumstances are unpredictable and sudden changes have to be made).

Major issues in *Twelfth Night*

1. Feasting versus sobriety
Twelfth night is the last day of Christmas feasting, and the play is often described as a 'festive comedy', written specifically for performance on that festive day. In the comic sub-plot there is a straight clash between

those who support feasting, eating, drinking, and general sensual enjoyment (Sir Toby, Feste, Sir Andrew, Maria), and Malvolio, the puritan figure who stands for sobriety, caution, and restraint. Malvolio is humiliated at the end of the play, but those belonging to the other group are also punished. Feste is condemned for his involvement in the Malvolio plot, Sir Andrew has his head broken, and Sir Toby has to get married quickly to avoid retribution. It would seem likely that Shakespeare is not prepared to give either viewpoint his total support, and that although he tends towards the party of feasting and fun, it is with the reservation that they too have things to learn.

2. *Self-knowledge*

Self-knowledge is perhaps the most significant theme in *Twelfth Night*. At the start of the play only Feste and Viola have a reasonable degree of self-knowledge. Orsino believes he is in love with Olivia, but the falsity of this belief is shown by the fact that when they finally do meet they are arguing within a few seconds. Orsino never goes to meet Olivia, but sends messages to her through others, and it is the idea of being in love that attracts him. His lack of self-knowledge means that he cannot come to a realistic appreciation of anyone else's character. It takes most of the play for him to realise that he is really in love with Viola. Olivia believes her desire to withdraw from the world is a result of grief at the loss of her father and brother, whilst in reality it is fear of a cruel world and a desire to lock herself away from danger that prompts her. She does not realise this about herself, and so is defenceless against the first person (Viola) who dares to challenge her and present her with a slice of the real world. It is a subsidiary theme of the play that those who do best in life are those who face it and live it to the full, not those who try to hide away. In a tragedy Olivia's lack of judgment would lead to her death; as it is, she has to suffer, but is allowed to fall in love where that love can be met by someone who will prove a true husband to her.

Malvolio lacks self-knowledge, and hence knowledge of others. He cannot see that he is only a steward, and thus can deceive himself into thinking that Olivia really is in love with him. It is not so much a question of Malvolio being duped and trapped by Sir Toby and Maria; rather, it is his own vanity that stops him from perceiving the truth, until it is cruelly but comically forced upon him by his enemies.

Viola knows herself, but chooses to adopt a disguise and thus cover her real nature from the world. Understandable as this is, it is still held to be a fault in a play which demands complete honesty about oneself. As a result of her self-imposed disguise Viola is forced to agonise about the apparent impossibility of her love for Orsino ever being recognised, and is forced by her loyalty into the unenviable position of acting as marriage broker and go-between for the man she loves. Olivia's falling in love with her is merely another added complication, but one which reinforces the message that honesty about oneself is the only sure way to avoid the problems of relationships.

Feste has a shrewd insight into his own nature and that of others, but is condemned to be the Fool, whilst he is probably the most perceptive character in the play. He knows himself, but it is open to argument whether or not he can control himself over his hatred for Malvolio. When Viola says 'Disguise, thou art a wickedness/Wherein the pregnant enemy can do much' she is pointing to the central issue of *Twelfth Night*: people who disguise themselves – from themselves, or from other people – are courting disaster. Self-knowledge and honesty are the oil which causes the wheels of society to run smoothly, and which allow people to live in harmony with each other.

3. *Time and age*

It is possible to see *Twelfth Night* as being a play about age. It requires no manipulation of the text to play Feste as relatively old, and this fact alone would allow him to be shown as a man who can no longer keep up the deception necessary to pretend he is a Fool, and not the wisest man in the play. Feste sings, very pointedly, a song about the loss of youth to Sir Toby, and again it is very easy to suggest that Sir Toby is a man whose feasting and riotous behaviour are part of an attempt to persuade himself that he is still young, a vain attempt to turn back the clock. Maria could be an aging spinster, seeing in Sir Toby a last chance of marriage; and their marriage at the end could be a recognition on both their parts that their youthful, carefree days are over. Orsino could also be seen as being in his mid- or late-thirties, his frantic wooing of Olivia a desperate last attempt to persuade himself that he is still young, still the youthful lover who can throw away the cares of state and be totally consumed by passion. Viola, Sebastian, and Olivia represent genuine youth in the play, and the final sequence of marriages reflects the fruitful joining together of the ages – one 'old marriage' between Sir Toby and Maria, one 'young marriage' between Sebastian and Olivia, and one mixture of old and young in Viola and Orsino.

Time is seen as a healer and a solver of problems, and partly also a symbol of the fact that humans cannot hope to solve all problems and issues instantly and on their own. Time is needed for all human endeavour to come to fruition.

Major questions in *Twelfth Night*

1. *Does Feste deserve his fate?*

Feste has aroused more comment than almost any other character in *Twelfth Night*. He is often played as a cap-and-bell jester, a witty and impertinent fool whose function in the play is to provide a frothy humour and word play to hurry along the action. The extent to which

Feste is played in a lighthearted way is a matter of major concern. It is possible to see Feste as someone embittered by the knowledge that he alone is the wise man. In this view, he is in danger of losing his job at the start of the play, and being thrust out into 'the wind and the rain'. He saves his job by a hair's breadth, but is shown to be more and more restless as the play proceeds. When given the opportunity to humiliate Malvolio, the man who has most humilitated him, Feste cannot resist the opportunity, and taunts Malvolio mercilessly (and far more than the occasion warrants) as the priest Sir Topas. When the plot is revealed it is the final straw for Olivia, who gives Malvolio's letter to Fabian to read. This can be taken as a sign that Fabian is to be the new Fool in Olivia's household, and that Feste has been rejected. The play's final moments have Feste, left outside the charmed circle of marriages at the end of the play, singing the sad and poignant song 'The Wind and the Rain'.

It may be that Feste is more serious than he appears at first sight; but how much can any director afford to present only an embittered Feste? If this is done, there is the risk that the play's sombre side will be emphasised to the exclusion of the comedy, and the play will be made more tragic than it merits.

2. Sir Toby: amiable extrovert or dangerous egotist?

As with Feste, there is a debate as to the extent to which there is a dark side to the character of Sir Toby. On one side there is the fact that he usually appears as a large, jovial drunkard, a man whose only object in life is to have a good time, and who only resents interference with that aim. On the other side he does seem to offer a threat to peace and order, rather like a scaled-down version of Falstaff; Malvolio may be justified in objecting to the riotous behaviour of Toby and his cronies. Seen in this light, Sir Toby manipulates and uses Sir Andrew and Maria for his own ends, and is a thoroughly selfish, and even dangerous, presence in the play. At least one production has had Sir Toby as a thin, composed, and youngish man, more akin to Edmund in *King Lear* than Falstaff.

3. Malvolio: justice or outrage?

Malvolio is thoroughly humiliated in *Twelfth Night*. He is made to look foolish in front of his enemies and his employer, locked up, treated as a madman, and generally made the recipient of much crude humour. At the end of the play he announces that he will be avenged on all those present, and this call for revenge has been seen in some quarters as a justifiable response to an unfair situation.

Malvolio gives every appearance of being a good steward. There is no suggestion in the play that he is dishonest, or that he mishandles Olivia's affairs and her household in any way at all. Sir Toby and his cronies are clearly making a great deal of noise when Malvolio interrupts them, and it is obvious that in so doing he is at least in part carrying out Olivia's wishes. In fact it could be argued that Sir Toby and the others are grossly unfair to Malvolio, someone loyal to his mistress who is only doing his job as he knows best. He falls for a well-planned and well-executed trick, only made possible by the treachery of one of Olivia's closest servants; with such skilled help it is no wonder that he is fooled. His being locked up as a madman is an unnecessary humiliation, an additional and unmerited cruelty. He is, in fact, 'much wronged' in the play, punished more than he deserves, and the cause of a sour note being struck at the end.

On the other hand, Malvolio seems to enjoy the position of relative power he has over Sir Toby, and to enjoy actively the task of stopping other people from enjoying themselves. He is a typical example of petty officialdom, someone who struts around when given a uniform, and imposes his authority on those under him. He is ludicrously vain and wrong-headed to consider even that Olivia might marry him, and possibly lecherous along with it; and it is his own vanity and pig-headedness that condemn him to be humiliated. Alone of the major characters in the play he lacks the capacity to learn, and the final insult which he hurls at the other characters is merely testimony to a mind so hardened in its vanity and arrogance that it cannot be changed, even by the total humiliation it receives. In effect, it can be argued that Malvolio gets what he deserves.

As a passing note, it should be remembered that the Elizabethans were less sensitive to cruelty than the modern age. In a time when teeth were pulled out without anaesthetic and bear-baiting and cock-fighting were major sports, the treatment of Malvolio might not have seemed as harsh as it could do nowadays. Malvolio can perhaps also be seen as a representative of the Puritan sect, a branch of Christianity much mocked in Elizabethan and Jacobean times for its harsh attitude to pleasure, and – which may be particularly relevant to Malvolio's treatment – its condemnation of the theatre and plays.

Observation and conclusions

Plot and sub-plot
Twelfth Night is another play with a well-defined and technically well-conceived plot and sub-plot. The main plot of the play concerns Olivia and Orsino with Viola, whilst the sub-plot, primarily comic but throwing light on the play's main themes, centres on Sir Toby, Sir Andrew, and Malvolio. The linking characters are Feste and Viola, although the real link is that the sub-plot all takes place within the household of Olivia.

Illyria
It was once fashionable to talk and write about the 'magic' world of

Illyria, and suggest that in *Twelfth Night* Shakespeare was creating a land of fantasy and magic in which dreams came true and only good things happened. Modern criticism is more likely to point out the underlying harshness in the play, and its essential closeness to reality. However, the festive nature of the play, the extent to which it is a celebration of human happiness and love, must not be under-rated. The more sombre elements in the play do not dominate it, but merely give a little perspective and colour to the happpiness that is the play's main concern.

As You Like It

General points

As You Like It was written at roughly the same time as *Twelfth Night*, that is between 1598 and 1600. It is sometimes suggested that *As You Like It* was the earlier of the two plays, as its tone is slightly lighter, but there is no firm evidence for this.

Wedding: it is sometimes suggested that the play was written to celebrate a wedding, or to be performed at one; this suggestion derives largely from the number of weddings there are in the play.

Songs: the play also contains a relatively large number of songs, which occur at regular intervals but which are not always linked very closely with the text, or what is happening on stage.

Major issues in *As You Like It*

1. *Self-knowledge*
The links with *Twelfth Night* go deeper than mere chronology. Both plays have the acquisition or search for self-knowledge as central themes; both have a female heroine who dresses up as a man, provokes self-knowledge amongst the other characters, and finally marries the man she loves after having deceived him for a considerable span of time about her real identity. The majority of those who come to the Forest of Arden acquire some degree of self-knowledge, this applying even to the evil Duke Frederick. As in all Shakespeare's other plays self-knowledge is the essential ingredient for a stable and productive society.

2. *Love and marriage*
Love, marriage, and self-knowledge are closely linked in the play. There are four marriages at the end of the play: Rosalind and Orlando, Celia and Oliver, Phebe and Silvius, and Audrey and Touchstone. To an extent each marriage says something about the nature of love and

marriage, as it works down the social scale from top to bottom. Orlando has to be educated out of his hyper-romantic notion of love, and brought into the real world, the only world in which a successful marriage can operate. Oliver has to be weaned away from self-love, which in his case has taken the form of ruthless selfishness and hatred of his brother. Phebe needs to be taught to love the real person and not the sometimes false image they present, whilst Silvius needs to be brought down to earth rather like a lesser Orlando. Touchstone and Audrey are a recognition of the physical nature of relationships between the sexes, and a reminder that its influence can never be dismissed or ignored; however coarse it may be, their relationship does at least have the virtue of honesty, and perhaps honesty is the prime virtue of all in *As You Like It*. As always in Shakespearian comedy there is also the figure of the person who cannot adequately give or receive love, and who is left out of the charmed, magic circle of lovers at the end of the play: Jacques is there to add pathos and melancholy to the play, and hence realism.

Marriage is a symbol in the play for the perfect union of mind and body which is known as love. Shakespeare points out that love can only grow properly where each individual knows him or herself, and can thus accurately judge other people: self-knowledge leads to accurate knowledge of others, and love can only proceed from accurate knowledge. The physical disguises and deceptions that the characters adopt are a visual symbol of the inner disguises that people erect round themselves, the barriers that have to be broken down before people can communicate adequately. The capacity to give and receive love is identified as a major virtue in the play, and it is a virtue even when it operates on the lowest of levels, as with Touchstone and Audrey.

3. *The play as a failure*
For so successful and popular a play a suprising amount of adverse criticism has been directed at *As You Like It*. It has been said that the play is full of casual workmanship; lacking in unity; full of 'padding'; and that it has a feeble opening and a slipshod ending. Rosalind is said to dominate the play almost to the exclusion of any other character, and she retains her male clothing long after the need for it has gone. There is virtually no action in the Forest of Arden, and very little action of the comic, boisterous type that proves so popular in Shakespeare's other plays (the orchard scene in *Twelfth Night* is an example). It has also been said that the concluding masque is not necessary, and that the introduction of Hymen strains credibility and adds a new note and tone to the play at a stage where it is too late to present it convincingly. It has also been argued that Duke Frederick's repentance and the marriage of Celia and Oliver are facile, unbelievable, and unconvincing.

It could also be argued that characterisation and themes are given more prominence and attention than action in the play, and that, far from being casual, the plotting is deliberately relaxed to allow greater concentration on characters and issues. Rosalind can be seen as a triumph, and the most compelling of all Shakespeare's heroines, and her disguise as a symbol of the themes of appearance and reality and of self-knowledge. Convention can be called upon to explain away the repentance of Duke Ferdinand and the marriage of Celia and Oliver. Perhaps these two incidents and the appearance of Hymen and the masque at the end of the play all fit in to a scheme whereby the play slowly sheds some of its more realistic elements to become more magical, more like a fairy story at the end.

Basic questions in *As You Like It*

1. *Why is Rosalind a dramatic success?*
In some respects it is surprising that Rosalind has received so much praise from critics and from theatre audiences. She treats Phebe harshly (after all, she is not to know that Rosalind is a girl), seems to treat her father with casual indifference, and makes some distinctly unmaidenly jokes about sexual matters. However, it seems that these features merely serve to make her more human, more real, and to prevent her from becoming so good as to be both unbelievable and unattractive. The name she adopts whilst in disguise – Ganymede – was that of Jove's page in classical mythology. The Elizabethan audience (or some of them) would have associated this name with the combination of intelligence and rational thought, the capacity to be joyful and rejoice, and the ability to give wise council; there is therefore a lot in the name that explains Rosalind's attraction. She has courage and determination, and can act on her own initiative. She defies convention when she dresses up as a man, but it is a convention we can do without for the duration of the play. Her independence is attractive. She has a great fund of common sense, but also a sense of fun: she knows when to laugh and when to think, and her thoughts go to the heart of a matter. She can love just as fiercely as Orlando, but she can do it without his excessively romantic attitude. She has a man's courage and a woman's patience. She is naïve and lacking in experience, but is somehow always in control of whatever is happening to her. Her combination of innocence, shrewdness, and a sense of humour has proved a very strong attraction to theatre audiences over the centuries.

2. *What is the importance of pastoral in the play?*
Pastoral literature is literature that concerns country or rural life. In the sense that much of the action of *As You Like It* is set in the Forest of Arden it is a pastoral play. Pastoral literature was classical in origin, and based round shepherds whose job – it was believed – allowed them to sit around on hillsides with ample time to sing songs, write poems, and

engage in love affairs with shepherdesses; the occasional necessity of fighting off a lion or other beast intent upon attacking the sheep provided some extra excitement. The Forest of Arden is a pastoral retreat in the sense that it is rural, relatively primitive, and as such brings characters closer to nature and their origins. However, Shakespeare's pastoral world is not simply a rural retreat, nor is it made an excuse to propound sentimental ideas about the beauties of nature. It is clear that the courtiers in the forest are subject to cold and hunger; the realities of nature are emphasised by the graphic destruction of a deer and an equally graphic account of Jacques' reaction to the killing. Wild animals threaten Oliver; Celia shows clear signs of boredom in her rural retreat. The pastoral setting does, however, provide a platform for debate on topics such as pastoral romance, and the merits of court and country, and the opportunities thus provided are used to the full by Shakespeare. However, it is a clear theme of the play that realism and honesty are virtues; whilst not actually mocking the pastoral convention the play uses it, and pokes slight ridicule at its excesses. Life has peace and violence, happiness and misery, wherever one looks in Shakespeare, and the pastoral retreat of the Forest of Arden is not allowed to be any exception to this rule.

3. *What is the dramatic function of Jacques and Touchstone?*
Jacques is melancholic. Part of his function is to act as someone who satirises and shows up other characters' folly; he has sharp words to say about Orlando and his romantic fervour, and about Touchstone and Audrey. However, he is also there to reveal his own weakness, the folly of melancholy and cynicism. The world of *As You Like It* is one in which characters who take their own future into their own hands (Rosalind, Orlando) are much preferred to those who are content to sit and moan, or who lack the capacity for direct action. Jacques laughs at other people's folly, but the ending of the play shows that he has become a prisoner of it, dependent on living in a faulty world to feed his own image and feeling of superiority. His melancholy and cynicism have become like a strait-jacket; he cannot free himself from their restraint. He must remain in the forest, alone, isolated, and melancholic, incapable of truly giving or receiving love.

Touchstone is a coarse Fool, providing a very basic physical type of humour for the audience. He does quite a lot to save the play from sentimentality; his wit, earthiness, and general crudity bring the play down to earth, and remind the audience of the real world of instinct and appetite. He is unusual as a Fool in that he gets married, and the marriage has aroused some critical controversy. In any event, it undoubtedly acts as a counter to the wholly spiritual love of Orlando, and provides the play with a wider spectrum of human nature. As with all the others who come to the Forest, Touchstone acquires a degree of self-knowledge, although in his case perhaps the knowledge he acquires were best left unresearched; Touchstone finds he operates on a base, physical level, but, sad admission though it is, it still provides a wealth of humour in the play.

Observations and conclusions

Women in trousers
As in *Twelfth Night*, a boy actor is dressed up as a girl pretending to be a boy almost as soon as the plot allows. The result is a wealth of irony, considerable comedy, and a peculiar shifting of roles and identities which serves to emphasise the strength of Rosalind.

Disguise
As You Like It has one of the most complex expositions of a disguise plot in the whole of Shakespeare, when Rosalind dressed as Ganymede is mock-wooed by Orlando, with 'Ganymede' pretending to be 'Rosalind'. The fact that Orlando can be in such close proximity to his love and not realise it says something about the shallowness of his response, but something also about how easy it is to communicate badly with people, and fail to perceive their true nature.

Pantomime
It has been suggested that the play should be played as a pantomime, with little regard to realism; possibly a more plausible idea might be to see the play gradually changing from realism to allegory, and finishing on a fairy-tale note.

Robin Hood
It is generally believed that one reason why Shakespeare wrote a play set in a forest was that a rival company had had a tremendous success with a play about the outlaw Robin Hood, set in Sherwood Forest.

A Midsummer Night's Dream

General points

The play was written some time between 1593 and 1596; it may have been written to help celebrate a marriage (a claim that is sometimes made for *As You Like It*), but there is no firm evidence for this.

Sources: the play is unusual in that no direct source has been found for the story used by Shakespeare. Originality had little value in Shakespeare's day, and a readily identifiable source can be found for most of his other plays. Equally, it has been said that the play's source is rural superstition and folk tales, and that it needs no other base.

Major issues in *A Midsummer Night's Dream*

1. *Love*

Love is a theme in all Shakespeare's comedies, but the treatment of the theme is either more confused or more complex, depending on one's viewpoint, in *A Midsummer Night's Dream* than in any other comedy. There are times when love is a very serious business in the play. The love between Theseus and Hippolyta had its origins in a straightforward military conquest; Egeus seems very willing to bring the full force of the law down on his daughter if she marries Lysander instead of Demetrius, meaning either death or life in a nunnery; the squabble between Oberon and Titania puts the seasons on Earth out of joint. The most famous lines in the play – 'The course of true love never did run smooth' – suggest the theme of old age versus youth, that age will seek to deny young love, but that it is unstoppable. The subject of Bottom's play, the tragic story of 'Pyramus and Thisby', at least in its original form, is a reminder of how this unstoppable force of young love can go tragically astray, as Shakespeare shows in his *Romeo and Juliet*. If this is the serious side of love in the play, then the audience can hardly help but be aware of the fact that for much of the time love is presented as comic, even ludicrous. The four young lovers are excessive in their love, and behave in an extravagant way, even before the love juice starts being poured in the forest: the juice may be magic, and therefore 'unreal', but the greater excesses it produces are carefully placed at a time when the audience have already seen the lovers behaving stupidly. Even under the influence of a magic potion, the sight of Lysander and Demetrius changing allegiance so rapidly can hardly reassure us as to the strength of their original love; and this inconstancy is even seen in Titania's ludicrous passion for Bottom and his ass-head. Love can be serious in the play; it can also be a matter of delusion, folly, and irrationality, and at times appears to be being held to ridicule.

One answer to this apparent paradox is that it is perfectly correct and reasonable for a play to present two differing attitudes to love, just as in *Antony and Cleopatra* Shakespeare shows the same love in two very different lights. Another answer is that this contrast only appears difficult to reconcile when the incidents are taken out of context. Darkness and the forest place the audience in the 'dream' of the title, and in this dream world anything and everything can happen. A third viewpoint is that the play's statement about love is that it can be serious and full of meaning, as well as being foolish and irrational.

2. *The dream world*

In *A Midsummer Night's Dream* morning, or daylight, and the court stand for reality, reason, and sanity; darkness and the forest stand for magic, the suspension of normal values, and a dream world in which things seem to be real but are only apparently so. In this sense the play goes on a journey into the forest and all it stands for, and ironically it is the journey into the unreal world of the forest that gives the characters the sanity, insight, and self-knowledge that will allow them to make a success of their relationships in the real world. This is a form of sanity-in-madness that will be familiar to anyone who has seen or read *King Lear*, where madmen are the only ones with any sense, and only fools speak or see the truth. The forest is a dream world, peopled by fairies and activated by magic, but it is close enough to the real world to affect it, and to cleanse people of their delusions by exaggerating them. We might almost see the forest as being similar to some types of modern aversion therapy, where a patient is put off, say, drugs or cigarettes by being given an overdose of them: the sickness or revulsion they feel after this is a cure for life – or so the theory runs. The forest does not invent or create anything: it merely amplifies whatever was there already, and enlarges it, and by so doing helps cure people of their folly.

3. *Techniques of comedy*
Many of the standard comic devices are used in *A Midsummer Night's Dream*: foolish rustics make fools of themselves in front of sophisticated courtiers, lovers do and say silly things, and people are shown as behaving in irresponsible and irrational ways. However, one extra comic element is worth noting: the technique whereby incident is piled upon incident, as in the manner of a modern farce, until it appears impossible that things will ever become clear again. The sheer speed at which the play moves and incident follows incident is a major factor in its ability to make an audience laugh.

Major questions in *A Midsummer Night's Dream*

1. *Weakness of characterisation?*
It is sometimes said that the characterisation in the play, and in particular that of the lovers, is weak and insubstantial. Certainly, Theseus and Hippolyta seem conventional figures, and Lysander, Demetrius, Hermia, and Helena can seem to have little to distinguish them. On the other hand, Titania and Oberon can be commanding figures, Bottom is a comic masterpiece, and Puck is an invigorating and stimulating portrait. It can be argued that the lovers are characterised as much as they need to be, and that for them to fulfil their roles in the play a great deal of individual characterisation is not necessary. They are 'the lovers' much more than they are Lysander, Demetrius, Hermia, and Helena, and the aim in presenting them is to comment on lovers in general, rather than on any particular individuals. It could also be argued that too much detail in characterisation might clash with the magic and unreality in the play, and cause the audience to question it.

Audiences can accept magic if it takes place in a magical world (hence the need to distinguish between the court and the forest), but too much depth of characterisation might make the magic appear unconvincing.

2. *How are the two worlds reconciled?*
A Midsummer Night's Dream takes place in two settings – the court and the forest. It has a mortal, earthly group of characters, and another group consisting of fairies and spirits. In one world, young lovers can be threatened with death, and Queens are won by military conquest; in the other, love potions create temporary madness, and spirits can circle the earth in forty minutes. These two worlds seem irrevocably opposed and different. Several devices, however, are adopted to ensure that these two elements do not seem irreconcilable. The fairies are definitely superhuman, but they also have very human characteristics: they squabble over servants, fall in love, and play jokes on each other with every sign of enjoyment. Theseus and Hippolyta stand at one extreme, the 'human' end of the play, and Oberon and Titania stand at the other, the 'fairy' end, but all the characters travel between both worlds, the fairy and the human, thus uniting them. For example, the squabble between Oberon and Titania can affect the seasons on earth, and Titania can fall in love with a human being, both links which draw the two worlds together.

3. *How closely are comedy and tragedy linked in the play?*
A Midsummer Night's Dream is clearly a comedy; it ends happily, and the majority of characters achieve their desires at the end of the story. However, as in all Shakespeare's comedies, there are some distinctly non-comic elements in the plot. Lysander and Hermia are clearly running great risks when they elope, and Egeus is a convincing portrait of a father who would hand his daughter over to the law if she failed to obey him. Oberon and Titania's argument has repercussions of a potentially serious nature on earth, and all the fairies – Oberon, Titania, and Puck – have great magical power and little to control their actions, should they wish to turn that power to evil. Though the point is made that the fairies are not servants of evil, they are linked with Hecate and other witch-figures. Lysander and Demetrius argue bitterly, and at times in the play it is at least conceivable that both Hermia and Helena could lose their prospective husbands. For a considerable part of the play it can seem as if the love affairs in it will end like the tragic story of 'Pyramis and Thisby'.

To counterbalance these harsh and sombre elements Shakespeare ensures that Oberon is watching over all the activities in the forest, so that, with his ability to control events, there can be no real sense of danger. Just as his love juice causes many of the problems, so the audience assume that he has it in his power to stop the chaos which he has caused. The comic sub-plot is so harmless as to inject an atmosphere of fun into the play; the audience can hardly believe that truly tragic things will happen in a world which contains Bottom. The situations which the lovers find themselves in are so ridiculous that this too takes any tragic edge off their predicaments, and the overriding presence of magic in the play allows for any major problems to be solved without too much trouble. There is enough harshness in the play to suggest a real world does exist not far outside of it; it is never let through into the play in sufficient quantity to blacken it, or remove its comic flavour.

4. *What is the attraction of Bottom?*
Bottom is uneducated, foolish, and naïve, as are the rest of the Athenian workmen, but in many respects he is distinguished from them, and becomes almost the major character in the play. He has a vast enthusiasm for life, and is a natural leader, both features which make him attractive and distinctive. He has total self-confidence, however ill-founded it might be. Foolish he might be, but he is not that foolish. He has a native shrewdness that lets him see some things other men might not see. He also has a capacity for survival and to adapt that shows itself at best advantage in the forest. Effectively imprisoned in the forest by Titania, and placed in a remarkable situation that would drive a weaker soul to madness, Bottom responds with courtesy and considerable composure. He is practical, hugely self-confident, utterly egotistical, and excitable all at the same time. The audience can both laugh at or with him. He is one of the world's survivors, indestructible and effervescent. Most of all, he has the capacity to dominate a stage, be it the stage of his 'Pyramus and Thisby', or the real stage of *A Midsummer Night's Dream*.

Observations and conclusions

Plot
A Midsummer Night's Dream has four plots, of roughly equal importance, centred round (1) Theseus and Hippolyta (2) Oberon and Titania (3) Lysander, Demetrius, Hermia, Helena (4) Bottom and the Athenian workmen. The more normal pattern for a Shakespeare play is a single plot (*Macbeth*), main plot and sub-plot (*King Lear*), or parallel plots of equal importance (*Much Ado About Nothing*), so the existence of four plots demands considerable additional skill from the author to blend them together effectively. The result is a great potential for variety in the four plots, although there will always be close links between them. Theseus and Hippolyta are closely linked to the young lovers, and to Bottom and the workmen at the end of the play; Oberon and Titania are similarly linked to the lovers and Bottom. The only strands not directly linked are Theseus and Hippolyta and Oberon and Titania, although

certain hints are made that there have been relationships between the two pairs.

Rhyme and punctuation
The play is one of the few in which characters speak in rhyme, having the effect of making the events seem unreal and so reducing their tragic potential. It also contains a marvellous example of how punctuation can alter completely the meaning of a speech, in Quince's Prologue to 'Pyramus and Thisby'.

The unreal world
Perhaps the most remarkable invention in the play is the forest world, a world in which anything can happen, and does. By placing the forest firmly in the realms of magic Shakespeare gives himself a marvellous dramatic freedom, a world in which he can make anything happen, secure in the knowledge that he does not have to explain it in realistic terms, and can always return things to normal in daylight and the real world. Just as film makers used to use the concept of a dream to allow characters to undergo experiences that would not otherwise be credible, so Shakespeare creates a dream world in *A Midsummer Night's Dream*; as with all good dreams, it has moments when it comes disturbingly close to reality.

Much Ado About Nothing

General points

Criticism: the play has received relatively little attention from critics. This could be because it presents few problems for the reader or audience, or because it is a remarkably self-contained play that sets out to do its job with the minimum of fuss. It may also be because the play itself is rather insignificant, with relatively little to offer.

Intimacy: *Much Ado About Nothing* is very different from the other comedies such as *Twelfth Night* and *As You Like It*. Whereas these other plays exist in a world that is separate and cut off from the real world (Illyria or the Forest of Arden), *Much Ado About Nothing* is set much more in the everyday world, albeit that of a court in Messina. There is none of the stylised, romantic dialogue of *Twelfth Night*, *As You Like It*, or even *A Midsummer Night's Dream* in the play; instead the language is spontaneous, familiar, and easy. The audience are presented with a group of people who have known each other for a long time, are on familiar terms with each other, and who deal for the most part very informally with each other. Thus realism and intimacy are two of the most frequently used words in commentaries about the play.

Visual elements: *Much Ado About Nothing* is also a very visual play, with the masked ball and the scene at Hero's tomb relying heavily on visual effects for their impact.

Major issues in *Much Ado About Nothing*

1. *Appearance and reality/self-knowledge*

The theme of appearance and reality is strongly underlined in *Much Ado About Nothing*, and, with it, the acquisition of self-knowledge. At the start of the play its world is a superficially happy one, but as is so often the case in a Shakespeare play, the appearance is deceptive. The extent to which appearance can hide reality is made clear by the masked ball, where one man woos a woman for someone else; just as Viola's disguise in *Twelfth Night* must be punished as a form of hiding the truth, so the use of disguise at the masked ball allows evil, in the shape of Don John, to enter and nearly cause an early breakdown of relationships. It appears that Hero has been having an affair; the truth is very different. It appears that Hero is dead; the truth is that she is alive. It appears that Beatrice and Benedick dislike each other; the truth is that their bickering and squabbling conceals a deep, latent affection.

People in the play must clearly learn to distinguish appearance from reality, particularly where it is the character of others that is in question. The point is then made that to learn the truth about other people it is first necessary to know the truth about oneself, and the characters have to be shocked into that realisation. Eavesdropping and overhearing play a large part in this – ironically, because deception here leads to self-knowledge. Claudio has to be shocked into not accepting things at their face value by the mock-death of Hero; Beatrice and Benedick have to be firstly tricked into realising their love and forgetting their pride, but must then also be shocked into a realisation of what love means. In their case, it means a command from Beatrice to her lover Benedick to kill Claudio; love is total commitment, to the death.

Much Ado About Nothing is a comedy; it lets people make their mistakes and live to profit from them and the self-knowledge they lead to; but, as ever, one character is left outside at the end, isolated by his incapacity to learn or to change. Don John must be taken away to prison at the end of the play, in recognition that reformation is not always possible. The theme is a simple one. Love is only possible in any real sense between people who truly know each other; people can only do this if they truly know themselves, and in order to gain this degree of self-knowledge it is necessary that they be tested and tried. Those with the potential for love will come through the ordeal happily, and much wiser; those that cannot must be locked away and denied the rewards and the happiness of love.

2. The nature of love

Various types of love are examined in the play, but the main division is between the romantic, conventional love of Hero and Claudio, and the eccentric love of Beatrice and Benedick.

Claudio and Hero's relationship is utterly conventional. Hero is an eligible and attractive young lady clearly destined to marry highly in the society of Messina; Claudio is an equally eligible and ambitious young man, and their marriage will satisfy them, their parents, and the demands of the society in which they live. Beatrice and Benedick's relationship, on the other hand, is unconventional, and quite likely to bring a flush to the cheeks of a society matron. They argue and fight, wound each other with words, and behave in an altogether unseemly and ill-mannered way. Yet their relationship is seen as being alive, true, and warm, and ironically they come to have a far better understanding of each other than do Hero and Claudio.

It would, however, be a mistake to say that all the credit goes to Beatrice and Benedick. Certainly, Hero and Claudio have much to learn: there is nothing wrong with their relationship, but it is too shallow, and must be deepened by true understanding and a greater degree of trust and faith. Claudio's problem is very simple: he is selfish. He has failed to make the major commitment of love, that one feels and thinks more for one's partner than for oneself, and so he sees what he believes to be Hero's indiscretion as a slur upon himself. Their marriage will be perfectly satisfactory, even if it lacks the spark and fire of Beatrice and Benedick's marriage. Perhaps the latter are so unwilling to fall in love because they do not like the conventional love affair as represented by Hero and Claudio; neither wants to slip into the conventional role of man and wife, seeing in this a loss of freedom and liberty. Yet here Beatrice and Benedick are at fault: they are so nervous about falling in love and submitting to the convention that they are blinded to an essential part of their nature, the need and capacity for love. They need to be woken up to this by their more honest friends. Benedick loses in his battles with Beatrice, in the meantime, because to fight her on equal terms would be to admit that she *was* an equal, which he can never do. Beatrice does not intend to do serious hurt by her remarks, but needs to learn that she can hurt. Intellectual pride is her sin, and she has to be educated out of it.

Thus the play points out the weaknesses of both conventional and an unconventional love affairs; what it never does is to deny the validity of love, or its prime importance in a society where living together is as necessary as the development of personal and individual qualities. Lovers can be very silly, as they are in *A Midsummer Night's Dream*, but they also possess an indefinable quality which can be thrilling and uplifting to observe.

3. *Interlinked plots*

The two plots in *Much Ado About Nothing* seem to be designed as parallel plots, of equal importance; but it is often stated that the Beatrice – Benedick plot dominates the play, and puts the Hero – Claudio plot in its shadow.

Certainly Beatrice and Benedick are immensely warm and attractive characters, and their encounters provide some of the funniest moments in the play. It could, however, be argued that to claim their plot as the dominant one is to disregard the actual nature of the two plots, in that each plot has a set of specific functions. Thus comedy and depth of characterisation are located in the Beatrice – Benedick scenes, whilst action is concentrated on the Hero – Claudio plot. Very little actually happens in the Beatrice – Benedick plot, whilst there is a wealth of action, almost melodramatic, in the Hero – Claudio plot. Thus all Shakespeare has done is arrange different aspects of the play into the two different plots. Beatrice and Benedick would not appear nearly as interesting if the relative inaction of their plot was not relieved by Hero and Claudio's affairs and dramas; conversely, the Hero and Claudio plot might lack warmth and depth of character if it were not for the presence of Beatrice and Benedick in the play.

Dogberry and Verges are sometimes seen as forming a third plot, and sometimes merely as an extension of the Hero and Claudio plot. They are there to provide the low comedy in the play, and their presence means that the play spans the social range from highest to lowest. Dogberry is one of the most famous users of 'malapropisms' in literature, a malapropism being the use of a word which sounds vaguely like the correct word for the context, but which is actually hopelessly wrong.

Major questions in *Much Ado About Nothing*

---

1. *How ineffective are Hero and Claudio?*

It can be argued that Claudio, far from being a hero of the play, is an unattractive, selfish, and callow youth whose behaviour makes the audience doubt his worth to be a husband to anyone decent or admirable. He appears to be considering marriage to Hero more as a matter of form than as a result of any true acquaintance with her. He lets someone else do at least a part of his wooing for him, and jumps to a hasty and wrong conclusion about motives as a result. He is hopelessly fooled by Don John, and treats Hero with vast cruelty by waiting until the moment of marriage to denounce her. He is still capable of joking and being flippant after the supposed death of Hero, and throughout the play the audience have difficulty in coming close to him, or even seeing if there is anything to know in him. Similarly, Hero is tongue-tied for most of the play and speaks only a handful of lines, is passive throughout the action, and says or does hardly anything beyond possibly looking decorative.

On the other hand, Claudio may simply be very young. His youth and inexperience are emphasised strongly throughout the play, and in its imagery. He is a friend of Benedick's, and this must count in his favour. There is no doubt he has performed most valiantly in the recent war. If he is fooled by Don John, then so are a great many people who are older than he is and, in theory at least, wiser. He is prepared to marry a woman he has never met, and who might be repellent for all he knows, in order to make good the damage he has done to Hero. It is also possible to argue that he is a conventional figure, the young aristocratic lover, and that the audience are told all they need to know about him: greater depth of characterisation is not necessary.

It may be that the Hero part was written for a very young and inexperienced actor who as a result was given very few lines. Again, a beautiful but frail and shy-looking actress should have no great problem in gaining at least some of the audience's sympathy, and if there is nothing particularly positive about Hero (with the one notable exception of her part in the arbour scene where Beatrice is tricked into declaring her love for Benedick) then there is nothing very negative either. As with Claudio, she is a figure of convention, and as such should perhaps be taken at face value, which is the only level the audience need. Perhaps Claudio does appear shallow at times; the final judgment must rest on whether or not the audience see enough to make them think that he can grow into a man, and change in the light of experience.

2. *How is the comic atmosphere of the play preserved?*

The bare bones of the plot of *Much Ado About Nothing* make it sound alarmingly close to a tragedy, and at certain stages in the plot it must appear as if that is what the play will turn out to be. A young woman is denounced at the altar, and dies; her best friend makes a leading character vow to kill the would-be bride's husband; an evil noble sows destruction and disharmony wherever he can – all this is far from comic. As it is, several devices are used to ensure that the play never takes on a tragic flavour.

Don John is obviously a major potential threat to the comic tone of the play. His potential for tragedy is defused in a number of ways. He is portrayed as the conventional villain, and audiences know that conventional villains tend to be defeated by conventional heroes, of which there is no shortage in the play. He appears alone with his henchman only twice and in short scenes, and thus is not allowed to overpower the audience with his evil. He talks about doing evil, but the audience never see him *do* any, which reduces his impact even further. We do not see the deception of Claudio, and only hear about it afterwards. The watch find out the deception almost immediately it has taken place. This does not stop the denouncing of Hero, but the audience know that the truth will be revealed eventually. Tension is increased by the audience not knowing when all will be revealed, but fear is lessened by knowing it will be revealed. Finally, Don John is not brought on stage at the end of the play in chains, but is merely removed from the action and placed out of sight, thus not threatening the comic tone of the play.

Dogberry and Verges also help maintain the comic tone. The audience feel that any society that can afford to have these two idiots as their policemen is not somehow going to have a serious crime problem, or be the type of society where real evil is allowed to happen. In effect there are probably only two moments, both of fairly brief duration, in which the play teeters on the edge of tragedy. One is where Hero does actually collapse, and for a moment the audience are free to feel that she really is dead; the second is when Beatrice asks Benedick to kill Claudio. Both these moments are swallowed up by the vast sea of comic goodwill that typifies the play, and dominates it. As with all Shakespeare's comedies, enough grit and harshness is put into the play to suggest the real world, and to make the audience appreciate even more fully the happy ending they are given.

Observations and conclusions

Much Ado About Nothing is famous for its comic characters: Beatrice, Benedick, and Dogberry. *As You Like It* and *Twelfth Night* are perhaps better known for their settings (the Forest of Arden and Illyria), and for their heroines, Rosalind and Viola – who are only partially comic characters in the sense of provoking laughter. It is up to the student to decide if this difference reflects a different level of seriousness between *Much Ado About Nothing* and these two other plays.

Antony and Cleopatra

General points

Problems: in many respects *Antony and Cleopatra* is a high-risk venture for Shakespeare. The majority of the audience would be familiar with the story, one of the most famous in history, and so he is tied to historical accuracy and has little freedom to alter the facts. Amongst other things, this means he has to have a considerable time lapse between the death of Antony and the death of Cleopatra, with the resultant risk of anti-climax for the second death; that he has to portray a tragic hero, so-called, who cannot even kill himself properly; and he has to stage a story that requires as an essential part of it a major sea battle – on the Elizabethan stage. As if to add to his difficulties, Shakespeare chooses to bring a clown or rustic on stage just before Cleopatra's death, who then proceeds to make a number of rather bad jokes about asps, something that logically should ruin the audience's sense of suspense for tragic *dénouement*. It is worth keeping in mind also that Shakespeare chooses a story that requires the ultimate in feminine charm and wiles to be acted by a young boy, on stage for almost half the play. Part of the interest of the play lies in seeing how these potential problems are circumvented masterfully by Shakespeare, in a play that is arguably without technical faults, and a masterpiece of dramatic craftmanship.

Tragedy and history: perhaps rather surprisingly the play is not normally talked of in the same breath as the four 'great' tragedies – *King Lear*, *Hamlet*, *Macbeth* and *Othello*. One reason for his might be the fact that it is a mixture of tragic elements with elements more often associated with the history plays.

Dealing as it does with a power struggle for the leadership of the Roman Empire, the play inevitably raises points of political morality and conduct. There is little to link the play with *Julius Caesar* by Shakespeare. Mark Antony appears in both, but the characters are very different, as are the plays.

Major issues in *Antony and Cleopatra*

---

1. *Rome versus Egypt*
The play presents a straightforward clash between two different and opposed philosophies and ways of looking at life. Egypt stands for luxuriousness, sensuality, indulgence, richness, warmth, pleasure, and a certain wiliness or trickery; Rome stands for power, efficiency, ruthlessness, and cold practicality. Cleopatra symbolises everything that Egypt stands for, Octavius Caesar all the values of Rome. Antony is caught in the middle, no sooner tied to one than he yearns for the other. Some idea of the stress that is placed on Antony is provided in the figure of Enobarbus, who has an essential symbolic role. Enobarbus is a Roman, and proud of it, but he is not immune to the charms of Egypt, as he shows when he gives a lavish and heartfelt description of the first meeting between Antony and Cleopatra. When it looks as if Antony is about to be defeated by Octavius, the Roman way of looking at things would have Enobarbus desert to the winning side, which is what he does; it is only practical and sensible to preserve oneself in this manner. However, there is enough of the Egyptian in Enobarbus to feel a huge personal loyalty towards Antony. Torn between love of himself and love for Antony, Enobarbus kills himself, unable to bear the strain of his

divided feeling. Antony is subjected to similar strain, and is also torn between the two worlds of Rome and Egypt. His strain is greater than that of Enobarbus, and he lives longer under it, which testifies to his greater strength and stature as a tragic hero.

One element of the tragedy is that neither Octavius, symbol of the Roman values, nor Cleopatra, symbol of the Egyptian, have right on their side. Octavius and the Romans are efficient, and they get things done, but it is hard to like them or to feel any personal warmth towards them. Conversely, Cleopatra and the Egyptians are hopelessly self-indulgent and impractical, but they do have the warmth and personality that the Romans seem to lack. One can admire and respect the efficiency of one set of values, and like and laugh with the other; what one cannot do is what Antony tries to do, which is to inhabit both worlds and both sets of values at the same time. They are irreconcilable, and, in attempting to bridge the gap between the two, Antony is hurled into the chasm between them. Octavius and the Romans win, as they seem inevitably set to do; one is left asking if the price for victory is not too high, and whether or not it might be worth injecting a little chaos into the world if by so doing one ensures the survival of people such as Antony and Cleopatra.

2. *Antony: Renaissance and Classical hero*
It is a cliché to say that each age produces its own heroes, and its own type of hero. Shakespeare has a natural tendency to present Antony as a hero of the type favoured by his own age, a type that could be described as the Renaissance, Christian hero (for a definition of the Renaissance, see pp. 58–9), but in fact Antony was a Classical hero, drawn from an age when the hero could and did have slightly different qualities. In some areas the two concepts are in agreement. Both Classical and Christian hero could have military skill, courage in battle, magnanimity, and single-minded devotion to duty, honour, and fame. However, the Classical hero was also often self-assertive, boastful and cruel, features which were definitely not a part of the pattern for the Christian hero. Shakespeare has to undertake a neat and delicate balancing act, presenting Antony as closely to the original as is possible, but steering clear of features in the original that would offend his contemporary audiences. The balance is not always an easy one, and the student should be able to perceive certain areas where there is an obvious strain between the two different definitions of heroism.

Major questions in *Antony and Cleopatra*

---

1. *The world well lost or the world ill lost?*
Just as there are two different philosophies of life in the play, so there are two different ways of looking at the love affair between Antony and

Cleopatra. Shakespeare's sources for the story, and a number of people in his own time, saw Antony as a fine man destroyed by his love, and brought to ruin through his own frailty and weakness for seeking pleasure. Seen from this angle, the love affair is a degenerate, corrupt, sensual affair, and it is sheer folly for Antony to abandon rulership for its sake. In this view, the world of power and influence that Antony loses to Octavius is a world 'ill lost', a world that should have been his for the taking had he not fallen under the spell of the witch-queen Cleopatra. This is one possible view of the love affair, sometimes referred to as the Classical view.

Another view, the Romantic, sees the love as something utterly remarkable, an experience beyond the normal run of human experience and precious enough to sacrifice worldly values for. Antony and Cleopatra may love only for a short while, and in so doing lose their chance of power beyond the wildest dreams of most people, but it is still worth it; all the power in the world cannot equal the power of their love, and the richness of life that it brings them. They achieve a nobility through their love that raises them so much above ordinary men as to render comparisons with conventional values irrelevant.

To a large extent this difference of opinion matches the clash mentioned above, between Rome and Egypt. Rome condemns the love, Egypt creates it. Rome is cold, inhuman, a place of intrigue, tactical struggle, and power politics; Rome could hardly be expected to praise something so human as the love between Antony and Cleopatra. Equally, there are times when the Roman view seems the right one. There is a sensual, corrupt element in the love affair, and Antony and Cleopatra, as with all lovers in Shakespeare, can be very silly in their behaviour. The difference between the silliness of these two and that of Lysander and Demetrius in *A Midsummer Night's Dream*, or Orlando in *As You Like It* is that untold death and destruction can result from the mistakes of Antony and, to a lesser extent, Cleopatra. Shakespeare seems to observe the situation, bring it to life, but fails to state a definite conclusion. At times the audience see Antony the mere 'fan to cool a gypsy's lust', but at other times we agree with Cleopatra that 'Eternity was in our lips and eyes'. In the final count, the audience and director make the final judgment on the relationship, not the author. The presentation of the relationship is a testimony to Shakespeare's honesty, his capacity to observe and present experience without showing the need to impose a meaning on it.

2. *What is the true nature of Antony?*

Antony deserts his wife and forgets his obligations in Rome in order to pursue a hotly sexual affair with a woman who has already seduced two notable Romans, Pompey and Julius Caesar, and who is thought of as a whore by most Romans. He deserts his second wife similarly for

Cleopatra, and then allows himself to be defeated by a man of half his years and experience who confesses that Antony is, or should be, the better general. Antony's defeat is caused in part by his ignoring good advice from those he should trust, and listening to someone who knows nothing about military matters. He then tries to make his servant kill him, and when this fails, his own attempt to commit suicide is bungled. All this suggests a man in his 'dotage', a figure sadly reduced in stature and skills, a pathetic replica of what he might be. He is inconstant, morally weak, blunt, clumsy in politics, and insufficiently ruthless or in control of his physical appetites.

On the other hand his affair with Cleopatra shows him to be a man who values warmth and friendship, and who can care for others as much as for himself. He admits to not being close to his first wife, and his second marriage is a matter of pure political convenience that is almost forced upon him. Cleopatra is stimulating and attractive, and Antony's defeat in battle owes as much to the weakness and treachery of the Egyptian forces as it does to any weakness on the part of Antony himself. He has a magnificent record as a general, is physically strong, and can be hugely determined. He has the ability to inspire vast affection and loyalty from all those he knows, and his servants in particular. Enobarbus cannot face desertion from Antony, but Antony is generous enough firstly to forgive Enobarbus and send all his treasure after him, and secondly to forgive Cleopatra the cheap trick (the false announcement of her death) that leads directly to Antony's own death. He has an unassuming directness and honesty that allows an audience to warm to him and forgive him many of his weaknesses. He may fail as a general and as a politician, but he succeeds as a human being, caught between two irreconcilable opposites, the values of Rome and the value of love. He has two prime virtues which ensure his survival: his military skill and his determination. The latter is diverted by Cleopatra, with the result that the former founders in the face of Octavius's skill. Antony could meet one opponent and still conquer, but he cannot conquer Cleopatra and Octavius. The result of his trying to do so is a dual loss: Cleopatra's life and his own.

3. What is the nature of Cleopatra?

The battle-hardened, cynical, totally realistic Enobarbus is driven to poetry by the sight of Cleopatra: 'Age cannot wither her, nor custom stale/Her infinite variety . . .'. She is characterised very little by physical description (possibly due to 'her' being played by a boy in the original productions), but rather by her moods. She is a creature of moods – excitable, stately, regal, girlish, curious, restless, flighty, childlike, experienced. Despite the conjunction of opposites in her moods, credibility is still maintained in her characterisation.

Cleopatra's status as a tragic hero can be compromised if the audience believe she is genuinely ready to parley with Octavius Caesar after the death of Antony. She flees from the sea battle, thus causing Antony to follow and lose the battle. She does not kill herself instantly after Antony's death, and when she does so it is by the easiest and most painless way possible. She appears to have kept back a portion of her treasure from Octavius, suggesting she intends to use it for herself and so live on. She does not appear to make up her mind to kill herself until she hears that Octavius intends to parade her through the streets of Rome in triumph, and thus her suicide is undertaken for the sake of her own honour, and not linked directly to Antony's death.

However, none of these episodes lead to any definite conclusion about her. She tries to kill herself with a knife, and is only stopped by one of Octavius's men. The apparent deception of hiding some of her treasure could easily be a ruse to lull Octavius into a false sense of security, in which aim it succeeds admirably. She clearly has a genuine love for Antony, and she does kill herself, quickly and effectively, talking mostly about her love as she does so.

As with the nature of the love itself, the decision about Cleopatra must rest with the audience and director; Shakespeare leaves it open, content to observe and report rather than conclude.

Observations and conclusions

Plot and poetry
The plot of the play is surprisingly thin, with comparatively little actually happening. This is part of the reason why the play is renowned for its poetry, and often thought of as the most poetic of Shakespeare's plays; in the absence of action, poetry and use of language take precedence and dominate the play.

Measure for Measure

General points

Problem plays: *Measure for Measure* is one of the so-called 'problem plays', in common with *All's Well That Ends Well* and *Troilus and Cressida*. The problem with all the plays lies in their tendency to try and match realistic characters with a fairy-story plot, and to impose a happy ending on a play which has shown too much of the darker side of human life for that ending to be convincing.

Major issues in *Measure for Measure*

1. *Justice and the law*

Justice is a clear theme in the play, although it is not always certain what conclusions about justice the play draws. The law is also inextricably intertwined with issues of justice, to the extent that the two can hardly be separated. Claudio has committed a sin in the eyes of the law, but in terms of common sense it is wholly excusable, and hence not a sin. Both Isabella and Angelo judge Claudio too harshly; Isabella comes to her senses, and Angelo has to become a sinner himself before he can understand the predicament of someone such as Claudio.

It is possible to see in the play a suggestion that all men are guilty, and that, therefore, mercy is a right for all people. This certainly helps to explain the leniency with which Angelo is treated, and the attitude of forgiveness towards Claudio that is evident almost from the start of the play. The need for mercy in a world in which all are guilty might also explain the condemnation of Isabella and Angelo's over-simple view of morality and judgment, and give an ironical point to the conflict which later develops between them.

In the hands of Angelo the law is something which all human beings must serve; but the play shows that it is the law which should serve all humanity, not the other way round.

2. *Self-knowledge*

As in almost all Shakespeare's plays self-knowledge is a theme in *Measure for Measure*. The Duke's departure and his disguise can be seen as a search for self-knowledge and enlightenment. Angelo and Isabella refuse to countenance the existence of sin within themselves; this only increases the danger that when it does appear, as is inevitable in any human being, it will catch them unprepared and will upset and dominate them totally. Only by an awareness of sin can its presence be surveyed and controlled; pretending it does not exist is no defence. Perhaps Lucio is condemned so heartily because he is a Malvolio/Jacques figure, the one character in the play who cannot attain self-knowledge, and so must be exiled and kept apart.

Major questions in *Measure for Measure*

1. *Can the contradictions in the Duke's behaviour be explained?*

The portrayal of the Duke is full of paradoxes and ambiguities. He hands over his kingdom to Angelo when he clearly has no intention of really departing, and will indeed be staying in the area for the duration of his supposed absence. He tells Juliet that Claudio will die when he knows that he will not, and he labours long and hard to convince Claudio that there is no escape from death when he knows that there is.

He lets Isabella believe that Claudio has been executed, and he appears to blame Juliet and Claudio for their misdemeanour, but at the same time encourages Mariana to go into Angelo's bed. He apparently feels no qualms about wedding the virtuous Mariana to a man who has attempted both murder and rape. The result of all this is that the Duke can appear as a manipulating, scheming, and heartless ruler who treats his subjects like puppets for his own amusement.

One answer is to suggest that the Duke should not be treated as a real character at all, but rather as a stage convention, a dramatic device used to bring about a happy ending. Another view is that he should be seen as a Christ or God figure, an allegory of Divine Mercy, and a living picture of how Divine Mercy operates first to observe and then to forgive erring and sinful mankind. A third view might state that the Duke does all he does first so that he can learn about humanity, and secondly to test and reform people by placing them in crisis and forcing self-knowledge upon them. Perhaps the Duke combines all three functions and roles.

2. *Should Angelo be forgiven?*

Angelo changes from being a symbol of righteousness to being the symbol of evil and desire in the play. He betrays the power and responsibility of the ruler, and the trust of the Duke. He has got rid of a perfectly respectable woman who loves him. He is prepared to be a total hypocrite, and plans to rape an innocent woman, bargaining with her for her brother's life. He then plans to kill that brother after having given his solemn word that he would not do so, thus ruining an innocent girl for nothing. In effect he is prepared to act in a totally evil and corrupt manner in order to satisfy an illegal, immoral, and wholly carnal lust. He is then forgiven his sins, and the audience are asked to believe in his repentance, the problem being that he goes unpunished for appalling crimes, and shows no particular sign of repentance.

It is perhaps possible to forgive Angelo his sins and share an understanding of him if he is portrayed as a man of iron will who has never allowed himself to consider the prospect that he might himself be sinful. When temptation does fall in his path in the shape of Isabella he cannot recognise his feelings as normal human weakness. Believing that he is uniquely sinful, and coming to terms with sin for the first time, he sees no option but to act as a devil incarnate and go the whole way with sin. He over-reacts through ignorance of normal sinful desires – a pointer to the essential nature of self-knowledge, and honesty about oneself.

3. *Isabella: paragon of virtue or despicable prude?*

At varying times Isabella has been seen as a marvellous symbol of virginal purity, and an utterly distasteful and self-righteous prude. The problem is that while it is theologically correct for her to value her immortal soul more highly than her brother's life, it is also distasteful, and an audience might prefer her to take a decision that was theologically and morally wrong, but more admirable in human terms, namely to sacrifice her body for her brother's survival. Perhaps Shakespeare's audience would have been more familiar than a modern audience with the idea that no good can come out of evil, and Angelo confirms this when he says he will not release Claudio even if Isabella does submit to him, thus perhaps justifying Isabella's early decision not to submit. A Jacobean audience would have had a more vivid concept of hellfire and damnation (which is what Isabella risks if she submits to Angelo), and would value the whole concept of honour more than a modern audience. However, it is dangerous to rely too heavily on assumptions about the Jacobean audience: being dead, they have the too-convenient attribute of not being able to argue with any features ascribed to them. Even if Isabella's decision is the right one, the play suffers drastically if she alienates the audience's sympathy.

Much of the problem can be resolved by the actress If she plays the confrontation with Angelo in terms of icy certainty she is liable to lose the audience's sympathy; if she plays it as a girl in a helpless and hopeless flight from defilement, someone convulsed by desperation, loneliness, and revulsion, then her decision not to give in to Angelo can be seen as springing from incontrollable aversion, something for which an audience can feel sympathy, and which increases their desire to see an end to the tyranny of Angelo's rule. Claudio and Isabella are essentially in the same position. Both are alone, helpless, threatened, and fearful, and in both this leads to selfishness. At the start of the play, part of Isabella's apparent sanctity is in fact selfishness, just as part of Angelo's morality is hypocrisy. Both characters have to change and acquire self-knowledge, with more difficulty than the corresponding characters in the comedies, but without the death and destruction that accompanies the acquisition of self-knowledge in the tragedies.

One problem that is less easily answered is the change that appears to come over Isabella mid-way through the play, when she seems to hand responsibility for her actions over to the Duke and lose much of her individuality, and at the end of the play when she rather surprisingly agrees to marry the Duke.

4. *A folk tale?*
Certain critics have advanced the idea that *Measure for Measure* is not a play based on conventional standards of reality and normality, but more of a fairy story or folk tale, and as such not problematic at all. Elements that were common in folk tales of Shakespeare's day are the idea of a ruler in disguise wandering at large through his domain; a priest who engages in plotting; substituting one woman for another in a man's bed, and basing a marriage on this trick; a corrupt magistrate who reforms at

the end of the story. The modern equivalent of such folk tales would be the fairy story, where the reader is expected to accept incidents that are unreal by normal, conventional standards, but which are sufficiently entertaining, amusing, or enlightening to be excused their unreality. Such incidents may also have a psychological realism even if they do not have a practical one: in 'Little Red Riding Hood' it is clear that by and large in the real world wolves do not dress up as grandmothers; it is also clear that little children feel threatened by things bigger and cleverer than themselves; but both child and adult can recognise the psychological reality of the events in the story whilst recognising the unreality of the incidents that bring it about. One can argue that the presence of folk tale elements in *Measure for Measure* signals the audience to suspend normal standards of disbelief, and accept the play on the level of psychological and emotional truths, rather than practical ones. If the audience know that in the folk tale all ends happily then the author can afford to delay the happy ending, and can invite the audience to marvel at his ingenuity in creating such a happy resolution.

This approach is less convincing if it is argued that some parts of the play operate on the level of a folk tale (the plot and the Duke being the main examples), whilst others operate on a level of gritty realism (the early characterisation of Angelo, Isabella and Claudio). The result can be seen as an awkward and ill-fitting compromise, with too much folk tale to allow the realistic passages to be effective, and too much realism to allow the folk tales to operate effectively at their natural level.

This links in with another frequent complaint about the play, which is that it is split down the middle. The first part is pure tragedy, exposing base human desires in a frightening and terrible manner; the play then undergoes a sudden switch into fairy story, where a benign Duke sorts out everyone's problems, and the main interest of the audience is diverted to seeing how well the author can resolve the chaos his plot has created. (*The Winter's Tale* is similarly split, but in a manner that most critics seem to accept as being successful.)

Observations and conclusions

Lucio and the low-life characters
The low-life characters in *Measure for Measure* are generally held not to be a success, being corrupt and seedy without any major redeeming qualities of wit or humour. Lucio is a particular problem. He has some fine speeches at the start of the play when he is acting for Claudio. His role is then suddenly changed to being that of a comic foil to the Duke, and then at the end of the play he receives almost the largest and heaviest condemnation from the Duke, apparently out of proportion to his real sins, and when a character such as Angelo is allowed to go free.

Performance
Despite its problems, the play is often successful in performance. It is sometimes suggested that the change that takes place half-way through the play is a reflection of Shakespeare having lost interest in his plot and characters; others have suggested that the problem lies in his becoming *too* interested in them in the first half, and exceeding the level of analysis proper for such a plot and characters. One image of the play is that it is like a large piece of cracked marble: damaged, cold, white, but shot through with dark strands, and beautiful and impressive even in its damaged state.

The Winter's Tale

General points

The Winter's Tale is unusual in that an account of a contemporary performance has survived. Dr Simon Forman, a quack astrologer and doctor, saw the play at the Globe on 15 May 1611. His acccount talks at great length about Autolycus, more so than any other character, and he does not mention the restoration of Hermione and the statue scene. This has led some critics to suggest that the statue scene did not take place in the original version of the play, or at least in the version that Forman saw; this is an interesting speculation, but can be no more than that.

The play has many features of the problem plays. It can be divided up into two almost separate halves, the first tragic and the second comic. The story has a fairy tale element to it, but the characters are relatively realistic. It has an ending that verges on the incredible, and it makes use of semi-miraculous incidents. However, the play is generally held to be a success, and it was probably the penultimate major play Shakespeare wrote, coming just before *The Tempest.*

Major issues in *The Winter's Tale*

1. *Time*
Time is a major theme in the play. Time is the great healer, although the point is made clearly that time cannot heal on its own; it needs human nature to complete the process. There is a distinct feeling in the play that all things change and are subject to time, that there is a natural progress in events that cannot be stopped, slowed down, or speeded up. This can be seen in the frequent use of imagery of the seasons in the play, and the cyclical nature of the plot. The existence of evil is never denied, but as in nature, nothing is ever totally destroyed, and all things can grow again, given time. There is a sense of the constant progress of time throughout the play, and by its final scenes Autolycus has sobered down, and

Hermione, Leontes, and Paulina are visibly much older: even the statue
has wrinkles.

Certain issues seem to matter less in *The Winter's Tale* than in other
Shakespearian plays. Leontes's jealousy is terrible and a sin, but it can
be forgiven without the necessity of his death, unlike the jealousy of
Othello. Human actions are compared to the four (or three) seasons,
and linked to them; the play can be said to start in Winter, and move
through Spring with the first sight of Florizel and Perdita, to finish at
high Summer. Implicit in this pattern is a threat, of course; autumn and
then winter must come round again in due course. However,
something – possibly Time, possibly Providence – seems to have human
fate and destiny under its control, and it is a force than cannot be argued
with or defeated. It can be harsh (Leontes and Hermione may survive,
but Mamillius and Antigonus die as a result of Leontes's jealousy), but it
is not as harsh as the force visible in the tragedies; it can be benign, but
not as benign as in the fairy tale world of a play such as *A Midsummer
Night's Dream*, in which all mistakes can be forgiven.

2. Interpretations of the play

The Winter's Tale has, for some reason, attracted a huge diversity of
critical response. Some early critics see the play as the product of
Shakespeare's 'serene retirement' in Stratford. In fact Shakespeare was
not so old when he wrote the play, and by definition was not retired if he
was still writing plays; we do not know if he was serene at that time in his
life, and even if we did it is always dangerous to draw too close links
between an author's life and his writing. Despite this, the view that the
play was written by a man in the autumn of his years has some value. It
points to the role of time in the play, and the belief that, given basic
goodwill, all things can be resolved by time. There is a desire for
reconciliation and forgiveness above all things, and this could be said to
be typical of the thought patterns of an older man. Another early critic
saw the play as showing Shakespeare bored with life, bored with drama,
and bored with everything except poetry. Any view that operates with a
total disregard of known facts and is rude about a great author is
attractive, but the poetry in the play, although different from much of
Shakespeare's writing (see Part 5 of this Handbook) is not particularly
remarkable, and for a bored man Shakespeare packs a remarkable
amount of excitement and action into the play.

Other authors were writing exciting but improbable plays in the latter
years of Shakespeare's life, most notably the duet of Francis Beaumont
(1584–1616) and John Fletcher (1579–1625). It is possible that
Shakespeare wrote *The Winter's Tale* to match the plays of his
contemporaries; it is also possible that they wrote in emulation of
Shakespeare. In Shakespeare's later years his company moved to the
indoor Blackfriars Theatre; possibly *The Winter's Tale* was written for

the more luxurious stage effects of this theatre, but Forman saw the play at the Globe, and it must have been designed, as were all Shakespeare's plays, to be acted in a variety of settings.

Some critics have suggested a major religious conversion on Shakespeare's part in the later years of his life, and that this is reflected in his later plays. A new set of moral principles does tend to emerge from the later plays, but that need not tie in with any religious conversion. More modern critics have suggested that the plays were written by Shakespeare in his dotage, as consolation for the harshness of an old man's lot. This would seem to link in with the earlier theory that Shakespeare wrote the play at a nadir of boredom, but again the theory relies too much on unproven biographical fact to be totally reliable. It is, however, appropriate to the dream-like quality of the play's ending, and the increasing level of improbability as the play progresses.

A final view is that the play is part of an experiment, although it is not always clear from critics who support this view what the experiment is in aid of. One attractive solution is that the late plays seek to combine the thoughts and outlooks of the histories, the comedies and the tragedies, in an attempt to produce a composite blend of experience that partakes of all views and outlooks.

3. *Plot and structure*
The play is slightly unusual, at least in terms of Shakespeare's earlier and middle plays. There is no single emotion at the heart of the play, it has no climax at the end of Act 3, and a large number of new characters are introduced in Act 3. In addition it has a tragic first half and a happy second half; Leontes and Hermione vanish from the middle of the play, and Perdita is hardly seen in the final sequences after she and Florizel have dominated the middle section. Despite this, the play is more tightly constructed than appears at first sight. Both halves of the play start with Camillo talking to another man about a happy male – female relationship that is about to be disrupted. At the end of each half there is a climax scene (trial and statue) which centres on Hermione, one featuring her death, the other her resurrection. The faults of the first half of the play are removed in the second half, and the oracle and the statue scenes give a taste of magic and the supernatural to both halves.

It is possibly more helpful to see the play as falling into three parts, rather than two. Some critics see the play as being divided up into three sequences of Hatred, Love, and Reconciliation and Serenity; others go as far as to name the three sequences Hell, Purgatory, and Heaven. Another standard division is between Winter, Spring, and Summer. All these say something about the play, and are worth considering.

4. *Hermione as perfection*
Hermione is often held up as a shining example of how to portray

goodness convincingly on stage. She is morally totally upright, but never a prig or a prude, and she has a sense of humour. She is dignified without ever being condescending, totally loyal without ever being compromised. She is made to suffer intensely, but in doing so reveals her courage, her tenacity, and her steadfastness. Some critics have been so inspired by her as to see her as a symbol of Christ; in less extreme terms she might be seen as a representation of the redeeming power of true repentance.

4. *Subsidiary themes*
Jealousy and evil are obvious themes in *The Winter's Tale*, although it is noticeable that all the evil in the play is self-generated – human beings are responsible for it, rather than any outside force or agency. There is something of a debate between Court and Country, although it is not carried very far, and that largely through the observations of Autolycus. Finally there is the Art-versus-Nature debate that has its strongest statement in the discussion between Polixenes and Perdita at the sheep-shearing festival, where the question is asked if Nature can be improved on by man or by itself.

Major questions in *The Winter's Tale*

---

1. *What are the weaknesses in the play?*
There are a number of contradictory, unusual, or unlikely episodes in *The Winter's Tale*. Bohemia does not have a shoreline, or deserts; the play is apparently set in a pre-Christian era, but it mentions the Emperor of Russia, the betrayal of Christ, Whitsun pastorals, Puritans, Christian burial, Giulio Romano (a Renaissance sculptor), all very much post-Christian references; it is not clear when it was decided to conceal Hermione, or by whom; it is difficult to see how Hermione's existence could have been kept a secret for sixteen years, and it seems strange that an immensely dignified person like Hermione would consent to the statue sequence, which is pointless for her and even humiliating; Paulina could not have known of the plot to kill Polixenes; Hermione says the oracle gave her hope that Perdita was alive, but she hears the same oracle as the audience and Leontes, and there is no direct mention of Perdita in this; the Shepherd and Clown should recognise Autolycus in his new clothes. These are minor areas of uncertainty, but certain scenes have aroused more consternation. Having Antigonus pursued and then eaten by a bear can seem very silly; the device of Time on stage can seem clumsy and far too obvious; the statue scene can be seen as improbable, unrealistic, and a mere gimmick on Shakespeare's part. There are also quite a large number of 'asides' in the play (where an actor turns aside from the others on stage and addresses the audience without the others seeming to realise). And why is it that Shakespeare does not show the scene in which Perdita is recognised as Leontes's daughter?

There are answers to most of these complaints. The exact whereabouts of Bohemia are irrelevant; it is just a name used to suggest a country that is not England. Shakespeare often uses anachronisms, and the inconsistencies of date and time are not noticeable on stage. As regards the bear, it is a symbol of violence, of which there has been a lot in the first half of the play; Antigonus's death has to be slightly comic because the play is about to move into a comic mode, and a tragic death might upset this. Time shows Shakespeare facing up to the problem of skipping sixteen years, and being totally honest about it, perhaps winning the audience through sheer daring as much as anything else. The statue scene can be effective drama, because at that stage the play is firmly in the realms of magic. Perhaps the recognition of Perdita is reported at second hand so as not to steal the fire from the statue scene: two emotional scenes in so short a space of time might demand too much from the audience.

At the heart of many of the so-called weaknesses is the issue of whether or not the play is more of a fairy tale than an attempt to emulate real life. If it is seen as partly a fairy story, then it is wrong to demand conventional standards of reality from it.

2. *Is Leontes's jealousy credible?*

Leontes's jealousy appears to burst in on the play unprompted, and to transform a loving husband into a jealous tyrant. There has been considerable argument over whether or not the jealousy has been brewing for some while, or whether it really is conceived and born in the space of a few lines in the scene where it first becomes obvious. One explanation of this sudden jealousy compares it to the eruption of a volcano: when Vesuvius erupted people did not stand around theorising, but simply tried to get out of the way. In other words, jealousy is like a natural phenomenon that defies logic and reason, and takes its own course in and out of the world, acting according to its own rules rather than those of humanity. More and more in Shakespeare's later plays the audience are asked to accept things which in the earlier plays they might have expected to be explained to them. Leontes's jealousy is a fact of the play, and it is presented with such total certainty that on stage the audience are too busy observing to wonder if they should be believing.

Observations and conclusions

The Winter's Tale presents rather than explains, and shows that human beings are subject to time and forces greater than themselves. In Autolycus it has a very successful comic figure, and one with a very long pedigree. Singing, witty rogues throng the Elizabethan and Jacobean stage, with Feste being perhaps the nearest direct comparison, and

Lucio in *Measure for Measure* perhaps a failed attempt to produce an Autolycus-like figure.

The Tempest

General points

The Tempest, like *The Winter's Tale*, is a tragi-comedy. One of its major themes is love, and it has much comedy and music in it, as well as a lavish masque, all of which are features generally associated with comedies. With the banishment of Prospero and the treachery that goes with it, Caliban's attempted rape of Miranda, and the unrepentant Antonio and Sebastian it has elements that would normally be seen as tragic, at least in potential. The play is therefore a blend of tragedy and comedy.

The play was probably influenced by a true story, in which a group of sailors were split off from the rest of their fleet by a storm and cast up on the Bermudas, islands well suited to sustaining life. The sailors survived to make their way back home again, and the excitement generated by the story of their miraculous escape may have been a factor in the writing of *The Tempest*.

The Tempest is Shakespeare's last full play.

Major issues in *The Tempest*

1. *Several themes*
In common with a number of Shakespeare's later plays, *The Tempest* does not look at one or two isolated themes but presents experience that relates to a wide range of issues.

Power and knowledge are themes. Prospero seeks greater knowledge but in so doing loses his power as Duke. Ironically, his knowledge is then turned into power, in the shape of his magic, and the plot points out the dangers of seeking too much power and too much knowledge. By returning as Duke and giving up his magic Prospero seems to strike a happy and healthy balance.

Authority and responsibility are looked at in the play, as is the conflict between civilisation and savagery. Mercy, forgiveness, regeneration and the healing power of time are also examined and presented. A major theme is that of love.

2. *Love*
As always in Shakespeare's plays, love is seen as a redeeming and highly precious force. Prospero loves Miranda, and bases all his plotting and his scheming round his concern for her. He is redeemed by the power of his love, and allowed to resume his authority partly because of it.

Miranda has the capacity much-valued in all Shakespearian heroines, that of falling in love at first sight, in her case with Ferdinand. For Caliban, love is a physical act: he plans the rape of Miranda and is only sorry he cannot carry it out; for this blasphemy he is left alone on the island at the end of the play, the familiar figure left out at the end of Shakespearian comedy, as if to remind the audience of the value of what they have seen. The marriage between Miranda and Ferdinand, innocence and continence, holds great promise for the future, and is a symbol of regeneration and peace after the storm, much in the manner of the marriage between Perdita and Florizel in *The Winter's Tale*.

The Tempest, perhaps, most of all stresses the features most likely to help an audience to make sense out of a world that teeters on the edge of anarchy and chaos. Love is one feature that can redeem life, and patience is another: Prospero must wait and strive for learning and self-knowledge before his wishes can come true and justice be done. Innocence and constancy, symbolised by Miranda and Ferdinand, and self-knowledge, of the type that will let Prospero give up his magic in recognition of the fact that it has served its purpose, are further such features. The play does not say that evil and unhappiness can be permanently banished by these positive forces: Caliban remains on his island; Sebastian and Antonio do not really renounce their evil: and no doubt Prospero could be ousted again from his kingdom if he let things slip to the same extent. The world has not changed, merely the self-knowledge and capacities of some of those who run it.

Major questions in *The Tempest*

---

1. *What is the significance of Prospero?*
Prospero is clearly the major and leading figure in *The Tempest*, the great conductor who orchestrates and leads the action, and causes it to happen in the first place. Prospero is a warning that we all have to live in the real world, however able we may be, and do our duty. It is not his seeking knowledge that damns Prospero and brings banishment to him, but that in seeking it he denies his responsibilities as a ruler. On his island he seeks and gains more knowledge of the kind that made him overlook his duties before, but he is rewarded for it this time by being returned to power because on the island his search for and use of knowledge is for practical purposes, amongst which is the fulfilling of his duty towards his daughter.

Prospero shows the audience that a man can never be divorced from his duty and responsibilities. Prospero also shows the healing power of time and the value of mercy and forgiveness: only a strong man could forgive Antonio and Sebastian, the power of mercy being strongly emphasised in everything Prospero does. Furthermore, he shows the value of love and its redeeming qualities. In some respects he is reminiscent of Oberon in *A Midsummer Night's Dream*, a man whose magic power places him above the realm of ordinary men. In another sense he can be compared to the Duke in *Measure for Measure*, as the ruler who sees and understands everything, and has power over all those he meets.

2. *What is the significance of Caliban?*

Caliban is a savage, but he raises a great many questions in the play. Prospero seems to treat him very harshly. Caliban welcomed Prospero to the island and showed him all its delights, only to find as his reward enslavement to Prospero, and being made a prisoner on what he sees as his own ground. It is tempting to see the relationship between Prospero and Caliban as reflecting the relationship between the coloniser (or imperialist) and the native of the land colonised, with the native helping the newcomer only to find himself enslaved as a result. Equally, Caliban brings about many of his own problems by attempting to rape Miranda, and being wholly unrepentant about so doing. Perhaps Caliban shows what man is without the benefits of civilisation and self-denial. In this view Caliban represents basic mankind, the rapacious and unthinking bundle of primitive instinct that lies at the heart of all humanity. Such instinct needs to be controlled, restrained, and disciplined, so that the finer points of man – reason, rationality, constancy, love – can emerge. Prospero is thus the voice of civilisation and order, Caliban the pit of savagery that awaits us all once we lose or forget the standards of civilised behaviour.

Some critics have seen in Caliban an essentially sympathetic character, perhaps even a symbol of oppressed minorities the world over. This is perhaps to look at him through rose-tinted spectacles. If he is oppressed and a prisoner on his island, it is because he poses a direct and proven threat to innocence, in the shape of Miranda. Caliban is a threat to decency, safety, and all civilised standards, because as a savage or 'salvage' he cannot do one of the things that distinguishes man from the animals, namely control emotion, instinct and immediate gratification by means of rationality, thought, self-discipline and control.

3. *Is the play a fairy tale?*

The Tempest is often described as a fairy tale. It has human beings and spirits, handsome princes and beautiful princesses, people cut off from the real world, magic, and the triumph of good over evil. It is difficult not to see the play as a fairy tale when banquets disappear instantly, magic wands are made and broken, and strange old men summon up storms and tempests to oppress the wicked.

However, the temptation to see the play in this light needs to be restrained. It is in fact a remarkable combination of fairy story and realistic representation. There is nothing fanciful or fairy-like about the deposition of Prospero, the political motivation of Antonio and Alonso, their murder attempt, or Caliban's attempt to rape Miranda. Ariel may be a spirit but he is called on to deal with human beings who are as mortal and as real as he is ethereal. Real time is used throughout the play. Some four hours elapse during the action, which, as well as being chronologically consistent within itself, all takes place on roughly the same spot. In terms of realism this compares very favourably with *The Winter's Tale*, in which five acts are sufficient to see Perdita conceived, born, and betrothed.

Observations and conclusions

The Tempest presents a diffuse, shifting, and complex set of values and ideals. It is the least simple of Shakespeare's plays, and yet can be one of the most rewarding; it is certainly persistently popular on stage.

Romeo and Juliet, Julius Caesar and *The Merchant of Venice*

Romeo and Juliet, Julius Caesar and *The Merchant of Venice* are not a group of Shakespeare's plays in the way that the four great tragedies, or the problem comedies, are groups. Where they are united is in their standing with critics and audiences. Each of the three plays is famous in its own right, but they tend to be set for examination purposes as individual plays, rather than as background reading or as plays representing Shakespeare's tragedies or comedies as a whole. As a group they stand somewhere between Shakespeare's acknowledged 'great' plays and his lesser works. They are also linked in that each play tends to be associated in the mind of the non-specialist reader or audience with one particular scene or episode, such as the balcony scene in *Romeo and Juliet* ('O Romeo, Romeo! Wherefore art thou Romeo?'), the murder of Julius Caesar in the Capitol ('Et tu, Brute?'), and Shylock's demand for a literal 'pound of flesh' in *The Merchant of Venice*.

Romeo and Juliet

Romeo and Juliet was written comparatively early in Shakespeare's career, and, great work though it is, it does show signs of immaturity and lack of control on the part of the author. There is no sub-plot or relief from the main story-line; in itself, this is no bad thing and occurs in a number of other plays, but the play is also quite long, and this, coupled with frequent halts for lengthy soliloquies, can become tedious. There is great variety in the language of the play, but also occasional clumsiness and a tendency for the characters to become long-winded. There is perhaps rather too much word-play and punning for modern taste, and the huge number of coincidences upon which the plot rests can strain credibility. It is probably slightly less fair to say the same of the vast changes in characterisation that Romeo and Juliet undergo as the play progresses: in this respect the play demands to be treated as a romance, rather than a direct attempt to re-create reality.

The play's strengths are its language, and the central portrayal of the lovers, so much so that Romeo and Juliet and their love have become a part of folk-lore. As might be expected, love is a major theme in the play. At the start of the action, Romeo is in love with the idea of being in love, playing a game in the manner of Orsino in *Twelfth Night*. His meeting with Juliet sweeps away the false love and replaces it with genuine feeling, a feeling so strong that it eventually destroys the lovers. Here the play is firmly in the tradition of great love stories, such as *Antony and Cleopatra*, or *Wuthering Heights* (1847), the novel by Emily Brontë (1818–48). One difference is that in *Romeo and Juliet* Fate or Destiny seems determined to destroy the lovers, and they contribute relatively little to their downfall. (In Shakespeare's later tragedies there is more of a two-way relationship between Fate and the tragic heroes; Fate does not merely squash them flat.) Other attitudes to love covered in the play are the practical, down-to-earth attitude of Capulet, in which love is almost a business deal, and the attitude that sees love in almost purely sexual terms (the servants, the Nurse, Mercutio).

The play is also about hatred, typified and portrayed by the Capulet – Montague feud. It is almost as if the destruction of the two lovers is the price that must be paid for the cessation of the feud: the fact that peace is bought at the price of their destruction makes the ending of the play not wholly pessimistic, and provides an element of renewal and regeneration that is typical of tragedy.

Romeo and Juliet has a magnificent plot, and Shakespeare deliberately altered the story from his sources to make the action take place over a few days, rather than months. The effectiveness of the story can be gauged by its revival in the form of the extremely successful musical, *West Side Story*, set in a twentieth century urban jungle.

For the examination candidate the play can present particular problems, largely because of the huge reputation of the play on the one hand and its recognised flaws on the other. The answer is to take the play on its own terms. In moral or philosophical terms it is not as profound or probing as the four great tragedies, and it occasionally reveals a lack of control on the part of the author; on the other hand, the power of the story, the total commitment of characters and author, and the sheer single-mindedness of the play give it a remarkable power and strength.

Julius Caesar

If literature and Shakespeare's plays were dominated by logic then *Julius Caesar* would be required reading for any student studying *Antony and Cleopatra*, and *vice versa*. As it is the plays share only a Roman setting and certain character names; those characters who appear in both plays are given very different personalities in each.

Julius Caesar is famous for the assassination scene – the scene where Caesar, mortally wounded, gives up his fight against his murderers when he sees Brutus, the man he trusts, stabbing him. Written around 1599, it is a product of the mature Shakespeare, unlike *Romeo and Juliet*.

Occasionally critics claim that *Julius Caesar* is the first of Shakespeare's great tragedies, and that it also qualifies as one of the great history plays as well. A more reasonable view might be that, like *Antony and Cleopatra*, it tries to be both and is not wholly a success in either mode. The tragedies tend to focus on one, or at most two, central figures, the histories on whole societies. *Julius Caesar* is about the Roman Empire, ambition, and conscience, and also about inner conflict, but it lacks a central figure. Caesar is the subject of the play, but is killed relatively early on, and though Brutus then has more of the play than any other single character neither he nor Caesar quite achieve the stature of tragic heroes such as Hamlet or King Lear. The ebb and flow of fortunes, the high stakes, the battles are all invigorating and stimulating, in the manner of the history plays, but divided sympathy clouds the issues.

Shakespeare seems to have been very concerned to get his historical facts right in the play, and this might account for a slightly mechanical element which some critics have perceived in the plot, and for the fact that the language, though very 'correct' and often charged with a resounding force, can appear a little too formal and lacking in emotional depth.

Perhaps the most common question examiners ask of the play is whether or not it ought to be described as the tragedy of Brutus. Brutus is certainly a commanding figure in the play, caught between the conflicting demands of personal loyalty, conscience, and the good of the nation as he sees it, but he is also rather *dull*: a calm, brave hero showing all the virtues of endurance can be an unexciting stage presence. Opinion about Brutus has altered dramatially over the years since the play was written; some have seen him as the pattern of selfless idealism, but others have damned him in the strongest terms for his betrayal of his friend, Caesar.

The presentation of some of the other characters is also the subject of controversy. Cassius seems cast as a major source of evil in the play, but his capacity for friendship redeems him later on as the audience are shown his equal propensity for the most intense love and hatred. The success of Mark Antony in the play can be seen as a pointer to the weaknesses of the characterisation of Caesar and Brutus: Mark Antony is alive, warm, human in a manner that Caesar and Brutus often are not.

It may be that Shakespeare treated the story of Julius Caesar with rather too much respect; certainly the play is more historically accurate than many of Shakespeare's works, and the verse is more consistently formal and elevated. As with *Romeo and Juliet*, the plot is gripping, the language capable of rising to great heights, and the themes (politics, conscience, ambition) are highly relevant. If the play is sometimes seen as not being quite as powerful or effective as certain of Shakespeare's other works, this is hardly a major criticism, since the standard he set for himself is so high. It may be that Shakespeare wrote the play poised between two different forms of dramatic exploration, the history play and the tragedy, and shows the first sign of Shakespeare's mounting disillusion which finally emerged in a play such as *Hamlet*.

The Merchant of Venice

The Merchant of Venice is sometimes seen as a comedy, and sometimes as a problem comedy; either way, the student quickly becomes aware that the Shakespearian definition of a comedy is not simply a play that makes the audience laugh. *The Merchant of Venice* is one of Shakespeare's richest plays, yet one of his most enigmatic. It is dominated by the figure of Shylock, but that domination is no simple matter. Shylock has been seen as a condemnation of the Jewish race, and the evil villain of the play, a view supported by the known anti-Semitism of Elizabethan England. Other authorities have seen Shylock as the tragic hero of the play, an isolated, lonely and reviled representative of a much-wronged minority group, and a man 'more sinned against than sinning'. On the one hand he seems to be a slave to money, incapable of any of the finer human feelings, and determined to kill Antonio with a frightening and wholly immoral commitment to revenge. On the other hand, his offer of an interest-free loan can be seen as a plea for friendship from Antonio, his decision to take his pound of flesh an understandable response to the loss of his daughter and his jewels, and his hatred of Christians merely a return of the hatred he receives unfairly from them. His speech 'If you prick us do we not bleed?' is a central point in the argument that Shylock is a tragic hero; his knife-sharpening at the trial scene the central image of the view that Shylock is an outright villain.

The uncertainties in the play do not end with Shylock, Bassanio, the romantic hero, can be seen as marrying merely for money. The whole business of the caskets appears to plunge the play from bitter reality into romance in a disturbing and disjointed way (in this respect the play is best compared with *All's Well That Ends Well* and *Measure for Measure*). Portia can be a perplexing figure. The young woman dressed as a man who goes out and does daring deeds belongs to the realms of folk tale, and perhaps this provides the clue to how the play should be seen; as at least partly a folk tale, especially in the manner in which it talks of love. If Portia knows about how the law affects aliens attempting to harm Venetians in advance of the trial scene, as she apparently must do, why does she not reveal her knowledge in good time and spare everyone the agony of the trial scene? One answer, inevitably, is that this very agony purges the participants of the guilt and sin that brought them to trial in the first place, although it is not always easy to see what Antonio's sin is. Finally, the last act, with its lovers' quarrel and the episode of the rings can seem an anti-climax, although others may argue that it resolves the issues of the play and restores the balance at the end: the theme of hatred has been concluded in the trial scene, and the play would be incomplete without a similar conclusion of the theme of love.

The play examines the morality of money, and it is critical of the Christians in the play, as well as of the Jew. Antonio, Bassanio, Portia and the others have wealth and privilege at the start of the play, but not happiness: their misery and depression is commented on several times. What distinguishes right from wrong in the play, good from evil, is the capacity of Antonio, Bassanio and Portia to be generous and to love others as much as they love themselves. Both Shylock and Antonio are isolated, lonely figures, and critics have commented on the surprising number of similarities and links between them. However, despite his love for his daughter Shylock seems to be a man who has given up human contact in exchange for the love and possession of money. As such his punishment – humiliation, a heavy fine and the loss of his daughter – can be seen as just, even if it might appear harsh for modern tastes. A similar complaint of over-punishment can be made in the case of Malvolio at the end of *Twelfth Night* and Lear in *King Lear*, one in the midst of comedy and one at an extreme of tragedy. If nothing else this points to a different idea of justice in Elizabethan times, perhaps harsher and more brutal than some modern concepts, but also more straightforward. The decision to play Shylock as a figure of hatred or as a figure of sympathy is one that actor and director have to face: the greatest actors manage to convey both attitudes simultaneously.

The Merchant of Venice appears to have many of the features of a problem play – most notably a happy ending that can seem to be at odds with the preceding action of the play – is certainly a dark comedy, but on its simplest level it conforms to the pattern of Shakespearian comedy, where those who are generous and can love are allowed to learn from their mistakes and live a fruitful life, whilst those without the capacity for generosity are cast out and isolated.

Part 4

Studying Shakespeare

An alphabetical guide to Shakespeare's style and technique

For the convenience of the reader various aspects of Shakespeare's style and technique are listed below in alphabetical order. Thus the student who wants an immediate definition of a soliloquy, or to know when and how Shakespeare used poetry as distinct from prose, can turn quickly to the relevant entry; the student who wants a general introduction to this aspect of Shakespeare's work can gain this by simply reading through all the entries. This is not intended as a complete gloss of Shakespearian terms, merely a brief guide to some of the more immediate topics of interest to examination candidates.

Act. Shakespeare's plays are usually divided into five acts, and these acts are themselves divided into individual numbered scenes. Much of this division is the work of individual editors, rather than being explicit in the original editions of the plays. The playwright Nicholas Rowe (1674–1718) was the first editor to divide the plays up systematically into acts and scenes, and to indicate locations for each scene; his six-volume edition of Shakespeare's works was published in 1709.

Various attempts have been made to work out a consistent pattern for the five act play, such as by saying that the first act sets the scene and provides background information, the second and third acts move the action forward at ever-increasing speed, the fourth act provides the turning point in the action, and the fifth act concludes the story with a fierce climax and provides the *dénouement*. Such theories are all fine and well, but they add little to the student's appreciation of the play (how many students can remember in which act Hamlet murders Polonius?) and are blown to pieces by the structure of a play such as *The Winter's Tale*.

Allegory. An allegory is a story or narrative, usually of some length, which carries a second meaning or relevance, as well as that of its surface story; and allegory is usually a method of telling one story whilst seeming to tell another. None of Shakespeare's plays are direct allegories in the sense that they seek to tell one story by means of another, but a number of his plays have been seen as having allegorical content. Possibly the most famous example is *Macbeth*, which has been seen as an allegory of the fall of man (the Adam and Eve story) that features in Christian doctrine. According to this Macbeth represents uncorrupted man, and Lady Macbeth the temptress or Eve figure whose action leads to their mutual destruction. Other plays, such as *The Tempest* or *The Winter's Tale*, can be interpreted on a number of levels, some of them allegorical.

Anachronism. A historically inaccurate episode or event. A famous example from Shakespeare's works occurs when a clock chimes in *Julius Caesar*; clocks had not been invented in Roman times, in which the play is supposedly set.

Apron stage. A stage or acting area that juts out into the auditorium, leaving the actors surrounded by audience on three sides. It is sometimes called a 'thrust stage'.

Bawdy. A term used to describe coarse, low, sexual humour or dialogue. Bawdy is usually the preserve of lower-class characters, but this can serve to make it even more startling when it comes from noble characters. Hamlet is obsessed with corruption, sexuality, and the 'rank sweat' of copulation. He is frequently bawdy, as when he says to Ophelia 'That's a fair thought to lie between maid's legs' and makes other suggestive remarks to her. Ophelia herself injects a strong sexual element into her speeches when she is mad, referring to the loss of virginity and physical relationships between the sexes. There are some extremely explicit speeches on sexual activity in *Romeo and Juliet*. Sexual jealousy and fascination with sexuality infests almost every line Iago speaks about Desdemona in *Othello*, and he announces the marriage of Desdemona to Othello by telling her father that a black ram is 'tupping' (having intercourse with) his white ewe.

Bawdy, however, comes in more frequently where one might expect to find it, in the low-life characters. It can range from the rather ominous Porter in *Macbeth* complaining about how drink increases sexual desire but ruins sexual performance, to the pathetic affair between the aged Falstaff and the diseased whore Doll Tearsheet in *Henry IV Part 2*. To the shock and horror of some editors, Shakespeare examines life in all its aspects, and he does not fight shy of being explicit about sexual matters where it seems necessary. It is possible, as some critics have suggested, that Shakespeare's own attitude towards sexuality was to see it as a dangerous corrupting influence, but it can also appear in his plays with straightforward good humour and even enjoyment. More often than most Shakespeare's bawdy is there simply because bawdiness is there in life as well, and Shakespeare is above all an honest writer.

Blank verse. Poetry based on a metrical structure (a repeating pattern of stressed and unstressed syllables) which does not rhyme. Shakespearian blank verse usually has five stressed syllables per line, though the structure can be very loose. As a general rule, the nobler the characters the more likely they are to speak in blank verse rather than prose. Coarse or low-life characters never use verse, but noble characters do sometimes use prose for less elevated or dignified scenes. Blank verse can be used to heighten effects or the mood of speeches, and to add weight and dignity to what is being said. Its rhythm can give an air of formality if it is regular, or suggest the breakdown of order, or of a human mind, if that regularity is suddenly broken. In the hands of an expert such as Shakespeare blank verse can become a remarkably subtle tool, and be used to reflect or evoke a wide range of moods and feelings.

Catharsis. The effect of tragedy upon the audience: a purging of the emotions of pity and fear by their presentation on stage.

Chorus. This word can have two meanings in Shakespeare. The first derives from Classical times, where the Chorus were a group of actors on stage throughtout the play who provided a running commentary on it. Shakespeare adapts this technique in *Henry V*, producing a single figure who appears on stage at irregular intervals to fill out details of plot and setting in the mind of the audience. In a less formal sense critics often refer to individual characters as having a chorus-like function. One example is Enobarbus in *Antony and Cleopatra*, whose presence and remarks act like a commentary on the actions of the main characters.

Comedy. In its original sense this meant simply a play with a happy ending, and this is the reason why books cast in a traditional mould refer to such plays as *The Merchant of Venice* or *Measure for Measure* as comedies; the term comedy is not used to imply a play which makes the audience laugh, merely one that ends more or less happily. Another aspect of Shakespeare's style is the manner in which he mixes comic and other effects, as for example at the end of *Antony and Cleopatra* when a 'clown' brings in the snakes with which Cleopatra will commit suicide. This is the last moment one would expect an author to start to make his audience laugh, just prior to the tragic climax of the whole play, but the scene works magnificently in relaxing the audience so that they respond to this climax with even more concentration and attention that would otherwise have been the case.

Shakespeare's ideas of what is and what is not funny can be a little strong for modern taste (the treatment of Malvolio is one example), and that his comedy can at times be of the type known as 'black comedy', as when a rather funny description is given of poor Antigonus in *The Winter's Tale* being eaten by a bear.

Effects. Shakespeare could make little or no use of artificial light in his plays, and for most of his career he was writing plays for a theatre which simply had a galleried, wooden wall behind the actors; painted 'flats' and extravagant decoration of the set were not used until later in the history of the theatre. What Shakespeare did have was music, discussed below in this section (see 'Songs and music'), and other sound effects which the plays suggest could be brought to bear on the audience with relative ease. Thus thunder and rushing wind, guns firing and the sounds of battle were available as sound effects. Just as in the 1982 London production of *Henry IV Part 1* actors provided animal noises for the yard of a country inn, so no doubt the actors of Shakespeare's company would have been similarly skilful in providing live sound effects. Costume blood, primitive make-up, and excellent costumes were other stage effects available to Shakespeare, as were the devices of a trap door and a curtained alcove from which spirits and ghosts could appear, and into which they could vanish.

Eponymous. A daunting word for a simple concept: an eponymous hero is a hero whose name is the title of the play, as in *Hamlet*, *Macbeth*, and *Othello*.

Fool. A large number of Shakespeare's plays contain parts for a fool or jester. Based on the medieval court jester, the fool or clown was a low-class entertainer with a licence to say what he felt like saying, even if it proved to be an embarrassing truth. The clown was much loved by the groundlings, or poorer members of the audience, and in *Hamlet* much of Hamlet's instructions to the actors presenting the play within the play concern the clown and his tendency to extemporise and generally try to steal the show from the more serious actors.

The variations possible within the broad role of the fool are revealed by the very different actors that are known to have taken these parts in Shakespeare's day. His first clown was the famous Will Kempe, a low comedian, and famed as a dancer, particularly of semi-indecent jigs. He seems to have been unpopular with the company and was not taken back into it after he tried, and failed, to dance over the Alps to Rome. Whilst Kempe was more a clown in the circus convention, the next clown was Robert Armin, a very different character and a very different actor. Kempe appears to have played the parts of Dogberry in *Much Ado About Nothing* and Peter the Nurse's man in *Romeo and Juliet*, but Armin played Feste and Lear's fool, both parts much more sophisticated, witty, pathetic, and musical than those written round Kempe. The fool or clown could thus be a relatively straightforward comic entertainer, probably appealing to the baser appetites of the audience; or he could be a wittier, sharper, and more effective stage presence, helping to point out truths in the plays and adding to their pathos and their humanity, as well as providing musical interludes.

History plays. The name given to those plays by Shakespeare which deal with specific periods of British history, and the aim of which is to explore political truths, rather than present a specifically comic or tragic vision of the world. The plays by Shakespeare most commonly classified as history plays are *King John, Henry VI Part 1, Henry VI Part 2, Henry VI Part 3, Richard III*, and *Henry VIII*, and the famous 'second tetralogy' consisting of *Richard II, Henry IV Part 1, Henry IV Part 2*, and *Henry V*.

Imagery. This word is used to mean a great many things by a great many critics nowadays, and perhaps the simplest definition is also the best. In its most basic form imagery is descriptive language; an image can be either a single word or a phrase, and imagery is simply the plural form used to denote more than one image. It is most often thought of as a visual picture, but an image can also relate to any of the four other senses (taste, touch, hearing, smell). More often than not an image is written in the form of either a simile or a metaphor. Shakespeare's imagery has been examined in the closest possible terms over the years, but largely as a result of the growth of new methods and techniques of criticism in the twentieth century. It has been shown that in certain of Shakespeare's plays the images used cluster around certain topics or ideas. Thus darkness, the colour red, and ill-fitting clothing occur again and again in the imagery of *Macbeth*; images of human flesh being pierced, penetrated, or tortured are very common in *King Lear*; corruption imagery dominates in *Hamlet*. Knowledge of the way the imagery is concentrated helps the reader to understand how certain moods are evoked in the plays, and may also give a hint as to the central 'image' of the play which Shakespeare had in his mind as he wrote it – the suggestion being that the author chooses images subconsciously to fit the mood of the play.

Irony. Irony signifies a word, phrase or episode that says one thing and means another; irony occurs when a word, phrase or episode has one surface meaning, and another contraditory meaning beneath its surface. It is ironical when Hamlet says that he is 'but mad north north-west', because he means he is not mad at all. This is *verbal* or *rhetorical irony*; a character says the exact opposite of what he or she actually feels.

Dramatic irony occurs when a character on stage speaks lines which have one meaning to him, and another completely different meaning either to the audience, or to the other characters on stage at the time. When Duncan remarks on entering Macbeth's castle 'This castle hath a fine and pleasant seat', the audience have just heard Lady Macbeth swear to kill Duncan that very night in the castle, so there is horrific irony in Duncan's praise of it.

Two notable examples of rich dramatic irony in Shakespeare's work are, first, when a boy actor playing a woman dresses up as a boy (as in *Twelfth Night* and *As You Like It*), and secondly, when the Fool, as in *King Lear*, is seen to be wiser than the supposedly rational character. A similar irony arising from the inversion of roles often emerges when a character goes mad in Shakespeare's play; in this state they often speak more sense than the characters who are supposedly sane.

Madness. Shakespeare used madness to suggest the breakdown of a mind that has been faced with greater strain than it is capable of handling. Mad characters appear in many of his plays, but it is the mad characters in the tragedies who have caught and held the most public attention: Lady Macbeth, Ophelia in *Hamlet*, and King Lear in a play which also contains the simulated madness of Poor Tom, or Edgar. Madness in Shakespeare does more than reflect the breakdown of all order and control in a human mind; by breaking through the bounds of convention it can give a character a new perspective and outlook on life, mad certainly, but often tinged with truths that saner people are too cowardly or short-sighted to recognise. Mad people have nothing to lose in saying exactly what they see and feel, as they have already lost everything in the eyes of society, and out of this freedom an ironical and perplexing vision of the truth can often emerge.

Malapropism. A type of verbal humour where a speaker substitutes for the correct word one with a similar sound but a wholly different meaning. Dogberry in *Much Ado About Nothing* is addicted to the use of malapropisms. (The word 'malapropism' derives from the character Mrs Malaprop in *The Rivals* (1775) by Richard Sheridan (1751–1816)).

Masque. A lavish form of dramatic entertainment relying heavily on song, dance and costumes, with extravagant spectacle and special effects. The final scene in *As You Like It* is sometimes said to be a masque, though whether it was performed as such is a matter of conjecture.

Pastoral. Literature concerned with rural life, and a simple, pastoral mode of existence. The best known example of pastoral in Shakespeare's work is probably *As You Like It*, in which much of the action takes place in the Forest of Arden.

Problem play. This term is usually applied to *Troilus and Cressida*, *Measure for Measure* and *All's Well That Ends Well*. It implies a play that has a happy ending, but which has sufficient harshness and potential tragedy in it to make that happy ending appear unsatisfactory or unbelievable. The characters in the problem plays are realistic, but the plot is often more that of a fairy story than one seemingly related to real life.

Rhyme. Apart from in the early plays, Shakespeare uses rhyme comparatively infrequently. He sometimes uses it to close a scene, giving the last character to speak in any given scene a rhyming couplet to end with. Rhyme can also be used in highly formal, magical or supernatural scenes, as with the Witches in *Macbeth*. It is also used to suggest bad verse or bad writing, as in the play-within-a-play in *Hamlet*. Characters who are pronouncing a moral, or a conclusion to be drawn from the action, sometimes do so in rhyme.

Romance. A term sometimes used of Shakespeare's later plays, such as *Cymbeline*, *The Winter's Tale* and *The Tempest*.

Scene changes. It is sometimes difficult to realise that in Shakespeare's theatre, with no set to change, scene changes took place with great speed, and there was hardly any time lapse between scenes. The result is that Shakespeare can frequently play one scene off against another, and gain significant effects of contrast by the quick changeover between scenes.

Soliloquy. A long speech in which a character, alone on stage, speaks his thoughts out loud.

Songs and music. Songs and music can play a vital role in Shakespeare's plays. Music has always been an attractive feature to an audience, as the popularity of musicals testifies, and the Elizabethan audience were no different. Songs can take many shapes and forms in Shakespeare's plays. The songs in *Twelfth Night* are very closely matched to the text, and make a direct comment on the characters and the action that is taking place at that moment. Thus Feste's first song in the play is about youth and how it does not last, and is sung directly at Sir Toby Belch, an ageing delinquent who is trying to drown the realisation of impending old age with drink. However, the songs in *As You Like It* seem to bear no relation to the text, and appear to have been put there simply to amuse and entertain. Similarly, the Witches' songs in *Macbeth* are so intrusive and out of character that most editors assume they were written by someone other than Shakespeare, and added in later. A different category of song is seen in the snatches sung by the Fool in *King Lear*, which are more often than not a satirical comment on the action.

As regards music, it was clearly used by Shakespeare as a stage effect. It signifies the presence of the supernatural in *Antony and Cleopatra*, probably announced the entrance of royalty in the processions so beloved of the Elizabethan theatre, and was a major device for suggesting the noise and tumult of battle. It has even been suggested that there was almost continual music throughout Shakespeare's plays, as is the case in many modern films or television serials, to add atmosphere and mood to the action. This theory still has to be proven.

Stage directions. It is largely a mixture of conjecture and educated guesswork that decides which stage directions in the original printed versions of Shakespeare's plays were included by him, and which are the product of later hands. For the most part, stage directions are very thin on the ground for Shakespeare's plays, with *The Tempest* being a notable exception. A number of stage directions are actually the work of modern editors, and it is always worth checking in whichever edition you are using whether the stage directions are from a folio or quarto edition of Shakespeare, or the invention of an editor.

Symbol. A symbol, like an image, is, something that stands for something else, but it is not merely descriptive. Symbols are multi-layered in their meaning, convey different things to different people. Thus the crown in the *Henry IV* plays is at one and the same time a symbol of sanctity and suffering, dignity and debasement, depending upon which character looks at it or wears it.

Tragedy. Originally, a play with an unhappy ending. For a more detailed discussion, see Part 2, pp. 43–7.

Tragicomedy. A play which mingles tragic and comic elements in its plot and characterisation, such as *The Winter's Tale* or *Cymbeline*.

How to approach a Shakespeare play

It is a bewildering experience to be faced for the first time with a Shakespeare play – especially if it is to be studied for an examination. It is frequently no less appalling the second or even third time round. There is the text itself – often difficult, obscure, and so laden with notes as to render it barely decipherable. Then there is the realisation that even a small bookshop will have a shelf full of texts of the play, anywhere between one and five different relatively short 'notes' on the play, longer critical introductions to the play, and a host of other impressive critical works on Shakespeare in general.

The first thing to try to do is to arrange to see the play. If you cannot see a professional production, see an amateur one; if an amateur one is not available, try to hire a video production. In any event, try to *see* the play before you *read* it.

The next stage is to read it. Never read criticism before you read the text, the only exception being in the case of a brief, accurate summary. When the language is difficult an accurate idea of exactly what is happening at any given moment in the play can be a decided advantage. It is better to read the play as it stands, without any critical help. It can also be very helpful to read a summary after one has read the play, to check that one's reading was accurate. If by the first or second act you are really confused over basic details of what is happening and to whom then consult a series such as *York Notes* for an accurate and reliable summary.

Once you have read the play, try reading something related to it. If you are studying *King Lear* then at least one of the other great tragedies is essential reading; similarly, if you are studying *Twelfth Night* you would be well advised to read *As You Like It.*

In the first instance, use a book such as this York Handbook to help you to find your feet in Shakespeare, but steer clear of other criticism until you have read the play and started to form some of your own opinions. Use critics firstly to check up on technical detail (stage design, the meaning of individual words and phrases), and secondly to start you off on your own thinking and conclusions about the play. *Always remember and cherish your first reaction to the play,* and only adopt the view of a critic if it genuinely seems to add to your own personal understanding of the play. Always put critics' views in your own words, to prove that you have understood them.

Part 5

The actor's Shakespeare

by PHILIP FRANKS

THE WORST PRODUCTIONS of Shakespeare's plays are without doubt those
of which it is said 'An ideal production for schools'. I have been more
bored in the theatre by Shakespeare's plays than by anyone else's, and
more infuriated. Yet he has also been responsible for my most profound
experiences in the theatre, both on and off the stage.

I was lucky enough to be taken to good productions of Shakespeare
before I ever came to study him, so I could not understand the waves of
boredom and apathy in the classroom, did not know why the plays
suddenly seemed dull, and felt deeply guilty after three hour's worth of
paper-rustling, sweet-throwing, and helpless giggling through a
production of *Macbeth* that I once saw on a school trip.

Perhaps Shakespeare should not be taught anywhere for five years, so
that a fresh view could be taken. So many people grow up with the
notion of an institution, a thing called 'Shakespeare', like algebra,
atomic physics, or smallpox. It is boring, it is full of hard words, and
stupid people. It is also full of Themes and Imagery, whatever *they* are.
Most of all you have to do it for examinations. If anyone manages to
enjoy Shakespeare at school they have to be some sort of freak, or very
lucky.

Of course, it would be nonsensical to claim that the academic
approach was worthless. The plays, as with any great work, yield
enormous riches under close analysis. An academic training does not
necessarily help an actor, however, and may put off a new student. It is
far more healthy to approach the play as a *play*, written for a wide
audience, and with all the freshness, vigour and variety of a new
age – written to be performed, to grip, to entertain, scare, confuse and
challenge the audience. There is no 'right' way to perform these plays,
although many traditionalists believe that there is ('school' Shakespeare
again), and there is no guarantee that the play will even mean the same
each decade. Changes in the political scene, in tastes, morals and fashion
may cause certain of the plays to be seen in a different light. I can
remember the ripple of shock that went through an audience as we
played *Henry IV Part 2* in 1982, and the dying King exhorted his son to
'busy giddy minds with foreign quarrels' – it was the day the Falklands
War started, and suddenly a whole political strand in the play leaped

into focus. Each play remains potentially vital and alive, waiting to be discovered.

As with so much else in society, the image of Shakespeare is still tarnished, in Britain at least, by attitudes towards the man and his work that were developed or current in the Victorian period, which was roughly the last half of the nineteenth century. The twentieth century has seen a theatrical revolution – not only with the advent of the electric stage light, but also with the advent of a single figure, the director. Prior to the advent of such non-participant 'guiding hands' as William Poel (1852–1934), Harley Granville-Barker (1877–1946), and William Bridges Adams (1889–1965) the company's leading actor would hire the scene-painters and costume makers, cast the play (around himself), and rehearse for about a week. The modern director does all these jobs, and a rehearsal period of four weeks would now be considered short. The power of the director is often challenged as being too great, but it seems to have rescued Shakespeare from a life in the library or the wax-works. By viewing the play through a prism (the director's vision) an audience is shown a *version* of the play, and actors are at liberty to make decisions and choices about the characters they play, instead of striving to portray some folk-memory of what they should be. As interpretative artists, this will naturally be more of a challenge and a spur to them to produce their best work, and a good director will thrive on his or her actor's ideas and suggestions so that the play becomes *theirs*. How much more exciting to see a production of *Macbeth* where all the thanes are characterised, where the Witches are different from each other, where there is a sense of a society turning sour, becoming violent, closing in, rather than a production where the cast consists of 'one star and twenty sticks', and they are all standing around in tartan shawls and Noggin the Nog armour.

A purist might make out an argument for letting the words speak for themselves, claiming that elaborate production or the wilful changing of the period of the play may cloud its meaning, as may swingeing cuts made at the director's whim. This can of course be the case. An American production of *A Midsummer Night's Dream* had Hippolyta locked in a bird-cage, Demetrius with a flashing neon jock-strap, a real lake, and a helicopter, none of which apparently illuminated the play very much. Even so, it was probably more fun than yet another *Julius Caesar* with everyone dressed in bed-linen, and at least it shows that someone had an imaginative response to the play. Perhaps it is true that a strong director can cloud an audience's perceptions, but generally the better the director the greater the area of the play illuminated.

Any actor faced with a new role must make a series of choices as to what his or her character is, what they want, and what they need. This is the process of discovery called rehearsals: not simply finding out where to move and how not to trip over the set, but finding out what *makes* you move and how you do it. Shakespeare, predictably, offers more choices than any other writer. This makes the plays rich and frightening to rehearse, and is one of the reasons why they are constantly revived and a constant source of interest to actors. There are as many ways of playing Hamlet as there are actors in Equity, the actors' union.

It is difficult – and with some almost impossible – to approach the plays with an open mind. Yet this should be the objective for the actor and director as well as the reader. 'Let the play happen to you' was Peter Brook's advice to his *A Midsummer Night's Dream* cast at the beginning of rehearsals for his famous 1971 production. He made the cast read the play again and again, more and more simply, to try to obliterate preconception. So wholehearted was this experiment that the play was finally, in performance, startlingly fresh and alive, divested of the clutter of stage tradition. He found a way of presenting magic that was credible and thrilling, using circus techniques such as trapezes, huge stilts and spinning plates, and discovered a method of staging (a bare white box, primary colours, a minimum of props) that made the audience listen to the play as if it were completely new. This was director's theatre at its best – a group of imaginative and talented people had worked as hard as they could to discover a play's meaning, under a powerful leader. What was shown was not a received idea of the play, nor was it a variation on it (as may happen with some directors), but a voyage of discovery into the play itself. I shall now try to illustrate with direct reference to some productions with which I have been involved how such a voyage might begin in rehearsals.

Henry IV Parts 1 and 2, Barbican Theatre, London, 1982

We met as a company, without all the parts finally cast, some months before the production was due to open. The director, Trevor Nunn, expounded some preliminary ideas before we read the play, saying that potentially it was a huge, sweeping epic, dealing with an entire country, with every level of society explored and a sense of crowding life that pervaded every scene. But also it was an intensely personal piece, could carry the sub-title 'Fathers and Sons', and was capable of detailed naturalism and intimacy. The artists with whose work he compared the Henry IV plays were Breughel and Tolstoy. We then read the plays. Even with the attractive image of a teeming panorama of medieval life in our minds, the plays still seemed remote and distant – even boring; people with place names instead of real ones yelled lengthy abuse at each other and a fat man told incomprehensible jokes. Also, apart from the battles, there never seemed to be many people on stage at any one time. Where was the teeming life?

We had to wait for the answer. The next step was an exhaustive analysis of the text; scene by scene was read, quietly and carefully, and then examined for any difficulties of language or obscure reference. The entire company was present at these sessions, not just those involved in a particular scene. There was some grumbling about 'being back at school', but it gradually paid the dividend that we all shared an easy familiarity with the language of the plays when practical rehearsals began. Parallel to this work the company had been given a set of research topics to tackle – different aspects of fourteenth-century and Elizabethan life. After a few weeks, these projects were presented to the rest of the group. Some were dull, some extraordinarily vivid: a description of London bridge in the fourteenth century, sounding like modern Hong Kong, gave us all a vivid visual image for the Cheapside scenes in the play: noise, variety, houses built up and up in grotesque piles, people crowded together, selling, eating, drinking, dying. We all felt clearer about what we might achieve in those areas. Another project on court protocol (the manners and etiquette of court behaviour) gave us a wealth of ideas for the court scenes; we had quick, potted history lessons on weaponry, battle strategy, medicine, the role of women, the price of fish, alcohol, the political structure of fourteenth-century England.

This large and rather unwieldy fund of knowledge was swiftly exploited in a number of improvisations, or rehearsals based on a theme or incident but without specific written dialogue, stage directions, or other instructions. The first and longest dealt with the first Boar's Head Tavern scene. Every member of the large company except those with lines to speak in the scene sat around for half an hour working out a character for themselves, consulting with others, and planning incidents. The stage management team filled the rehearsal room with tables, chairs, benches, step-ladders, barrels, stools, jugs, plates, tankards, money and weapons. At an instruction from the director the exercise began and apparent chaos ensued. Whores screamed and cackled; clients bartered and fought; drunks smashed tables or vomited; pot boys scurried everywhere with trays, slipping under legs, dodging between brawls; a country yokel was tricked out of his fortune by a card-playing con-man; stolen goods were exchanged for cash in an upstairs room; a government agent hovered menacingly taking notes. At another directional signal, the word spread that an *extempore* play was to be performed with one of the protagonists the Prince of Wales. The Hal and Falstaff actors began their scene very quietly and, in order to hear, the rest of the company crowded round as close as possible, nudging, giggling, fighting, breaking things. The actors who were playing the parts of Hal and Falstaff found they needed to grasp their audience: they became expansive, theatrical, crude, and were rewarded accordingly by boos, cheers and verbal abuse or encouragement. When the 'play' turns sour, and Hal rounds on Falstaff, there was a strong sense of embarrassment, even of danger and continued fascination – private events were being played out in public.

Suddenly the police arrived ('My Lord! The sherrif and a most monstrous watch are at the door!'), and chaos ensued again – criminals frantically collecting up their stolen goods, tavern staff trying to put the place to rights, whores scampering upstairs or haggling over unpaid bills, Mistress Quickly in a panic, Falstaff being bundled into bed, every corner stuffed with people hiding; then, finally, the entire clientèle sliding off into the night.

The exercise took several hours and was not a 'performance'; an outside observer could not have followed the plot. However, it captured an atmosphere that was vital to the scene, and a sense of society that was vital to the production. Hal's flirtation with the underworld can seem bland and childish at first reading. The Gadshill robber is, after all, fairly harmless, and Falstaff and his gang are never seen to hurt anybody. They could easily be presented as lovable, sub-Dickensian rogues. The disapproval of the King and his advisors therefore seems over-inflated and a major area of dramatic tension becomes weakened. What the improvisation showed was the huge importance of Hal's behaviour as a threat to his father's security as monarch. He became a public figure, whose every action was watched by society, judged and gossiped about. This idea was later intensified by the inclusion in performance of a group of street performers giving an impromptu scene from an anonymous Elizabethan work *The Famous Victories of Henry V*, a rather trashy piece of journalese which contains many of the incidents of the Henry IV plays. The scene was performed in the interval of Part 1, to the surprise and, I fear, confusion of most audiences that saw it. The Boar's Head improvisation also gave the company a sense of immediacy and danger that we tried (not always successfully) to retain throughout the production. It seemed important that Falstaff's world was a harsh one, unruly, anarchistic, frightening as well as seductive. Falstaff, as ruler of that world, would then appear more powerful – a genuine Lord of Misrule to threaten Henry IV's kingdom – not just the gullible old fatty of *The Merry Wives of Windsor*. The actors playing Falstaff's cronies explored dark areas of criminality and poverty, not easy comedy, culminating in a Pistol who emerged as a twitching, gun-waving psychopath as equally capable of blowing someone's head off as of rolling on the floor helpless with childish giggles.

These were all areas of the play which were illuminated by theatrical means. A similar process was applied to the other strands of the play – the political world of the court and the adventure story world of the rebels. The set (designed by John Napier) also made powerful statements about the world presented. Four huge, three-storey wooden structures, motor-driven, provided this set. They were capable of fitting closely together to suggest an intricate, ramshackle tavern; differently arranged, they suggested London streets or the galleries and corridors of a palace. For the battle scenes they disappeared completely, giving the illusion of a vast space. Whenever you looked at them you saw a different detail: they were studded with tiny religious pictures and crucifixes, and the upper levels were literally clad in armour – rusting breastplates, swords and spears were lashed on to make them bristle with military threat. A huge crucifix, on which the Christ figure was grotesquely twisted, leant against the set throughout. It is clear that what was striven for (and achieved) was a strong visual correlative to the action, not simply a decorative effect.

The set was immensely detailed, and this attention to detail was carried through the entire production. The King was formally divested of ceremonial garments and given a plain wool dressing-gown and a glass of water after his first speech; the transition from public face to private, lonely man was thus swiftly established. The inn at Rochester had crowing roosters, barking dogs, whinnying horses (all animal noises provided live by the company), as well as a bevy of ostlers, carriers and surly, yawning chambermaids. In Justice Shallow's recruiting scene in Part 2 great care was taken to evoke a sleepy rural village green in high summer, peopled by real men and women, not the usual collection of cretinous bumpkins. Feeble, the woman's tailor whose patriotism and high ideals startle even Falstaff, was later seen in the Galtree Forest massacre sparing the life of a rebel, only to be immediately cut down from behind. Wart, his pathetic friend, was then seen futilely dragging him to shelter.

These are a few examples of the way in which Trevor Nunn's original ideas were executed. The notion of a national epic looking at all English society was built up by the accumulation of these details. No character was too insignificant for attention; even a non-speaking soldier in Hotspur's army might be focussed upon – one, for instance, observed praying with a brass crucifix in his hand, obviously frightened, was comforted by Hotspur before the battle with his cry of 'Esperance, Percy and set on!' The same soldier with the crucifix was later seen in the battle leading an attack, shouting 'Esperance!' Later still the same soldier was cut down by Bardolph and Peto and his crucifix taken from around his neck. None of this is in the text, but it derives from the imagination of actors and a director responding to the text, and may serve to throw areas of the text into sharper relief.

My hypothetical purist might counter with the accusation that all that has been described is extraneous 'stage business'. There is a difference, however, between business and interpretation. A recent, and in most respects impressive Stratford production of *Much Ado About Nothing* began with a beautiful girl alone on stage playing a lushly mournful tune on a cello; very pretty, totally meaningless. The same production ended with another extraneous image of Beatrice and Benedick alone on stage deeply involved in an inaudible argument. Here the intention was clear and the play served; we were left with an explanation of their perhaps arbitary falling in love, which was that they adored *talking* to each other. This time the directorial intervention was resonant. The invention in *Henry IV* was for the most part similarly rooted in serving the play, and not merely for theatrical effect (although at best it achieved both). Occasionally it failed – the rebel scenes in both plays are extremely hard to make interesting or (in the case of *Henry IV Part 2*) even comprehensible, and these were not wholly successful. But at least it was a rich and fruitful production that made the plays live.

This production of the *Henry IV* plays was traditional in one significant way: it was dressed in something approaching correct period costume. Trevor Nunn felt that nothing was to be gained by lifting the plays from the period in which they were set. Many productions do make this change of period, however, and 'modern dress' is a regular source of irritation to the traditionalist.

All's Well That Ends Well, **Stratford-upon-Avon, 1981; London, 1982; New York, 1983**

As *All's Well That Ends Well* is not discussed in detail elsewhere in this Handbook, the following outline of the plot may be helpful. The Count of Roussillion has died. His son Bertram leaves his mother to become a ward of the terminally ill King of France. With him goes his friend Parolles. He is soon followed by the Countess' gentlewoman, Helena, who cures the King with knowledge gained from her late father. Offered any reward she wishes by the King, she chooses Bertram, who she has long loved, as a husband. He is horrified and soon abandons her, going to Italy with Parolles to fight in a local war. He swiftly distinguishes himself in the war, sending word to Helena that she will never be his wife until she wears his ring and carries his child. Helena, wandering through Italy as a pilgrim, arrives in Florence and learns of Bertram's passion for Diana, a local girl. She substitutes herself in Diana's bed and obtains Bertram's ring as a pledge. Meanwhile Parolles is exposed by Bertram's friends, the brothers Dumaine, as a cheat, liar and false friend. Bertram returns to Roussillion where he is confronted by Helena who is pregnant and wearing his ring. All ends well . . .

This production was directed by Trevor Nunn and set firmly and specifically in 1910. Work began with a similar intensive textual analysis to that applied to the *Henry IV* plays; a week was given over to workshops with the Royal Shakespeare Company's voice director Cicily Berry, before any specific work on the chosen production style started. *All's Well That Ends Well* is dubbed a 'problem play'. The reasons are many and various, but perhaps can be summed up thus: the almost fairy-tale convolutions of the story seem not to fit with the obsessively realistic characters, who can often seem so flawed as to be contemptible. Its language presents a related problem. Superficially conversational or even simple, it is on closer examination highly complex, full of difficult antitheses and precise intellectual ideas. Cicily Berry was concerned that we should find a method of using the language that was neither declamatory (the 'singing' style of verse speaking that some actors adopt) nor glibly modern – if the naturalistic conversational tone is too readily adopted much of the content is lost. The objective became to find a real reason for using the words we had to speak. This sowed some seeds that bore fruit in production; the exquisite formal wit of Lafeu, the superficial facility of Parolles, and in particular the various shifts in Helena from abject despair, to hard intellectual graft, to deviousness, to honesty, to an almost religiously inspired state – all these were found to be there in the verse. If an actor could find the true value of what he or she was saying, without trying too hard to impose an idea upon it, the character could suddenly become clear. This is a hugely difficult process, and only works occasionally, but was excellent ground work for the *All's Well That Ends Well* company.

The bare bones of a plot summary of the play suggest an improbable fairy tale, or worse, the sort of bawdy, pseudo-medieval soft-porn film beloved of European film directors of the late 1970s. What the summary leaves out and the production concentrated on was the minutiae of social detail contained in the play. The middle class characters are finely distinguished from the aristocrats, and feared as social climbers or praised for their own merits and skills. There is a sense of a world whose long-held social values are coming under attack. The chosen setting of 1910 (apart from begging the enormous question of why there was a King on the throne of France) made the social divisions in the play explicit and witty in a way that a traditional doublet-and-hose production no longer could. Parolles was always over-dressed. A lilac waistcoat, an orchid in his buttonhole, an evening scarf that was just too long – these small points established his pretensions more clearly than a similarly overblown Elizabethan costume would have. The severity of Helena's clothes made the same point in reverse. The brothers Dumaine also benefitted enormously; shadowy on the page, they became very precise emblems of the upper class that they have infiltrated; immaculately dressed for each occasion whether as early aviators in goggles and flying jackets or motorists in long leather coats they genuinely seemed to 'wear themselves in the cap of time, . . . eat, sleep and move under the influence of the most received star.' Their plotting against Parolles took on intriguing overtones of a social class closing ranks against an outsider. The social detail in the costume was carried through into the placing of each scene. Instead of 'a street' or 'a room' each scene was precisely set. A gymnasium-cum-riding-academy for the first scene at the French court sharpened the contrast between the dying King and the young lords around him and instantly gave Bertram a vision of a world irresistible to someone with his ambitions. The scene in which Helena cures the King was set in a gentleman's clubroom, all green baize, brandy, and cigars. Helena, with her overcoat and suitcase, became an outsider in the manner of some of the women in plays by George Bernard Shaw (1856–1950) – the New Woman in a male-dominated world. When at the end of the scene she quietly but proudly wheeled the King past a group of stunned officer cadets and elderly lords in tail coats, the enormity of what she was attempting became very real and immediate, not merely the clever trick of the fairy-story maiden.

The two short scenes in Florence were also transformed. In the first the Dumaines swap platitudes with the Duke, and in the second, Bertram is created general of the Florentine army. The first scene seems obscure, the second implausible. The solution was ingenious. The first scene took place on a railway station platform, with steam and platform announcements. A train arrived, disgorging new recruits, Bertram and Parolles (complete with golf clubs) among them. The Dumaine brothers, meanwhile, clearly late for their own train, were being buttonholed by an increasingly manic uniformed Duke. Their obscure speech became instantly clear for what it was – the devious language of diplomacy, the art of making nothing sound like something. The second scene also took place at Florence station, now obviously badly shelled and being used as an extemporary field hospital. Injured men lay on mattresses tended by exhausted and harrassed nurses. In a hastily erected operating theatre the audience saw (in silhouette) a man dying. A mournful harmonica tune subsided into silence as the Duke emerged carrying a bloody sword and looking even less rational or sane than before. He approached Bertram, writing a letter home at the front of the stage, and promptly created him general for the very good reason that he was the only officer left who was able to stand up.

Both these scenes are under half a page of text, yet capable of yielding theatrical riches. The changing of the period, here as elsewhere in the production, illuminated the text and themes of the play rather than clouding them. By being firm and specific about the social detail and the reality of the characters the director gave freedom to the actors to explore the complex, hidden motives of these characters. The world of the play made it clear where these people fitted, what was expected of them. When a character did not fit their mould (Helena's single-minded devotion, and Bertram's rejection of her are two examples) the effect was startling. The academic, study-bound notion of characters not 'fitting' their plot was hence given emotional, theatrical life. Instead of being the difficult and unsatisfactory play that many critics had described, *All's Well That Ends Well* emerged as a rich, bittersweet masterpiece – flawed, perhaps, and played in a minor key, but moving, involving, and fascinating.

Both the productions described above were large-scale works for big theatres. This is by no means the only way to see exciting Shakespeare. Many actors and directors prefer working in small studio theatres (theatres seating three hundred or less with the audience on three or sometimes four sides of the actors), where the design or scenic effects are minimal and the audience can be brought into closer contact with the play. This can be equally thrilling (Buzz Goodbody's *Hamlet* with Ben Kingsley, for example), and at best a studio production allows the actor a greater variety of expression. On a big stage the choices an actor makes must be very clear, and to a certain extent presented to the audience. In a studio swift changes of thought and verbal and emotional dexterity are more likely to 'read' to the audience. It is often sad to see an actor doing brilliantly detailed work in a rehearsal room which is then lost in performance because of the necessity to serve it up and perform. A studio production enables actors to hang out the detail they discovered in rehearsal, and, of equal significance, to relate closely to other actors without having to 'cheat out front' (facing the audience to say a line rather than the person to whom you are saying it) to be heard. Many large-scale performances of Shakespeare fail to reach the audience because of an uncertainty of purpose; the actor's thought is not clear and his or her voice does not therefore communicate. Studio productions can help actors to clarify their thought. You cannot lie in a studio; the audience is close enough to see every flicker and a lack of concentration or an unworked-out emotional line is instantly apparent. It is very easy to be adequate but dishonest on a large stage. It will not be interesting to watch but it will *pass*; the majority of school Shakespeare falls into this category.

In 1914 Harley Granville Barker said that 'for an actor to turn himself into a human megaphone was to miss the whole merit of Elizabethan verse with its consonantal swiftness, its gradations sudden or slow, into vowelled liquidity, its comic rushes and stops with, above all, the peculiar beauty of its rhymes.' The job of any actor in Shakespeare is to find the reason why that Elizabethan verse is used and then to use it with as much truth and wit and skill as he or she can. When it is used well it is a thrilling and accessible medium. When it is used badly, it is a deadening and distancing one. The answer is not to 'be Elizabethan' but to be Elizabethan and modern at the same time. Acting styles change, and each generation will have its own ideas as to how this fusion should be achieved. This is absolutely as it should be; the texts have yielded different riches, even different meaning, to different societies throughout history. The theatre must never become a museum.

Part 6

Select bibliography

Texts

All the editions listed are reliable, scholarly, and widely available. Remember that some examining boards stipulate which edition of the play must be used, but if you are free to choose your edition try to make sure that it is the correct one for your level of study.

ALEXANDER, P. (ED.): *Complete Works of Shakespeare*, Collins, London and Glasgow, 1951. This is the standard edition of the complete works of Shakespeare, and is deservedly popular. It has no notes on the texts, merely the plays and poems themselves, and a general glossary at the end.

Arden Shakespeare, Methuen, London. The New Arden editions have for many years been the standard texts for Advanced Level and University students; they have excellent introductions to each individual play, and are well annotated. However, certain newer editions, notably the New Swan series (see below) have tended to make the Arden texts seem rather dry and dusty, and Arden annotations are sometimes too brief on basic matters of translation and meaning, and too lengthy on textual problems and sources.

Kennet Shakespeare, Edward Arnold, London. These are excellent editions of the plays, aimed primarily at Ordinary Level students. Notes are carried opposite the text, translations and explanations are full and easy to understand (not always the case in Shakespeare texts: some editions print explanations that are more obscure than the original they were meant to explain), and layout is clear.

Macmillan Shakespeare, Macmillan, London. This is a relatively new series; soundly edited and reliable.

New Cambridge Shakespeare, Cambridge University Press, London. This is another famous edition of the plays; as with the Arden texts, the New Cambridge series is beginning to show its age a little, but it remains very popular with students.

New Penguin Shakespeare, Penguin Books, Harmondsworth. This is almost certainly the best-known and most readily available cheap edition of Shakespeare. It has good introductions, brief but useful notes on the text, and a higher standard of printing and presentation than many cheap editions.

New Swan Shakespeare, Longman, London. This series can be recommended unreservedly, and it is taking over from the Arden editions as the standard text for use by Advanced Level and University students. Each edition contains an excellent and wide-ranging introduction; annotations are printed on the opposite page to the text; the notes themselves range from very full translations of difficult words or phrases to detailed discussion of advanced points of criticism. Presentation is also excellent.

Players' Shakespeare, Heinemann Educational, London. A series very similar to the *Kennet Shakespeare* (see above), and excellent value for Advanced and Ordinary Level students, although the series is generally aimed at the latter range.

Signet Classic Shakespeare, New American Library, New York. Excellent value for money, these cheap paperbacks have a wealth of critical material and essays reprinted from other works, and adequate annotation, although this latter tends to be purely explanatory as regards meaning, and not critical in any wider sense. The one drawback is the poor quality of paper used, and the rather dingy layout and presentation of the text.

Swan Shakespeare, Longman, London. An edition published with a reduced vocabulary, for students whose native language is not English; useful in that area, but not recommended for examination candidates.

Background and biographical reading

Background and biographical studies of Shakespeare can be great fun, and add considerably to a student's 'feel' for the plays and the man who wrote them, but a certain degree of caution needs to be exercised in purchasing and reading them. Most of the books available tend to shuffle much the same information around in vaguely different orders, and the cost of such books often goes more on the wealth of pictures available than on their intrinsic worth or scholarship.

BADAWI, M. M.: *Background to Shakespeare*, Macmillan, London, 1981. Detailed background information, mainly aimed at the Advanced Level students.

BROWN, J. R.: *Shakespeare's Plays in Performance*, Penguin Books, Harmondsworth, 1969. A stimulating analysis and study of the plays in performance.

BURGESS, ANTHONY: *Shakespeare*, Penguin Books, Harmondsworth, 1972. Controversial, but stimulating and well-illustrated.

HALLIDAY, F. E.: *Shakespeare and His World*, Thames & Hudson, London, 1956. Another beautifully illustrated, well-written book, useful at all levels but not intellectually probing.

HARRISON, G.B.: *Introducing Shakespeare*, Penguin Books, Harmondsworth, 1966 (revised edition). Old-fashioned perhaps, but still probably both the best book and the best value in its field.

HUSSEY, MAURICE: *The World of Shakespeare and his Contemporaries*, Heinemann, London, 1971. Another lavishly illustrated and lengthy book; it tends to focus less on Shakespeare than many others of its kind, and relies heavily on its pictures.

SCHOENBAUM, SAMUEL: *Shakespeare: A Documentary Life*, Oxford University Press, Oxford, 1975, compact edition 1977. An admirable life.

TILLYARD, E. M. W.: *The Elizabethan World Picture*, Chatto & Windus, 1943, Penguin Books, Harmondsworth, 1972. This is *the* standard book on the intellectual and philosophical background to Shakespeare, and the author manages to make it much more interesting than it sounds. This book is essential reading. Most other books (including this present volume) rely heavily on it.

WELLS, STANLEY: *Shakespeare: The Writer and His Work*, Longman, London, 1978. An excellent, basic introduction to Shakespeare.

WILSON, JOHN DOVER: *Life in Shakespeare's England*, Macmillan, London, 1913. An anthology of contemporary material from Shakespeare's own time.

Critical series

Casebook Series, Macmillan, London. The Casebooks are collections of critical essays on one or more books. They are the best of their kind, but as with all such series the standard can be very variable, and prices high. It is wise to do a little preliminary reading before purchase.

Critical Idiom Series, Methuen, London. These are short books on such topics as *Tragedy* or *Comedy*, and are not specifically on Shakespeare. They are excellent value for the Advanced Level student.

Notes on English Literature, Basil Blackwell, Oxford. Sound, short critical introductions to individual plays.

Studies in English Literature, Edward Arnold, London. Lively introductions and guides to individual plays.

Twentieth Century Interpretations, Prentice-Hall, New Jersey. Collections of critical essays on individual titles.

York Notes, Longman/York Press, London. The best of the many series of notes available on Shakespeare's plays.

General criticism

BARRS, MYRA: *Shakespeare Superscribe*, Peacock Books/Penguin Books, London, 1980. This book is the product of a series of programmes run by London's Capital Radio on Shakespeare for examination candidates. It is great fun, at times very enlightening and at other times rather silly, but worth looking at.

CLEMEN, W. H.: *The Development of Shakespeare's Imagery*, Methuen, London, 1977. One of the pioneering works on Shakespeare's imagery; the second edition is the one given here.

GRANVILLE-BARKER, HARLEY: *Prefaces to Shakespeare* (4 volumes), Sidgwick & Jackson, London, 1945. Another pioneering work, these four volumes contain scene-by-scene accounts of various plays, by one of the leading directors at the turn of the century.

KNIGHTS, L. C.: *Some Shakespearian Themes*, Chatto & Windus, London, 1966.

PARTRIDGE, ERIC: *Shakespeare's Bawdy: A Literary and Psychological Essay and a Comprehensive Glossary.* Routledge & Kegan Paul, London, 1968.

ROSSITER, A. P.: *Angel With Horns*, Longman, London, 1961. A collection of essays on various plays, written with a marvellous sense of humour and considerable insight.

SPURGEON, CAROLINE: *Shakespeare's Imagery and What It Tells Us*, Cambridge University Press, London, 1935. The other pioneering work on Shakespeare's imagery.

Criticism: comedies and early plays

BARBER, C. L.: *Shakespeare's Festive Comedy*, Princeton University Press, Princeton New Jersey, 1959. Among other things this book explains Shakespearian comedy in terms of the various festivals of Elizabethan society.

BROWN, J. R.: *Shakespeare and His Comedies*, Methuen, London, 1957.

CHARLTON, H. B.: *Shakespearian Comedy*, Methuen, London, 1937. Slightly dated now, but simple and straightforward.

LEGGATT, A.: *Shakespeare's Comedy of Love*, Methuen, London, 1974. An excellent account of the themes and plots in most Shakespearian comedies.

MUIR, KENNETH: *Shakespeare: The Comedies*, Twentieth Century Views Series, Prentice Hall, Englewood Cliffs, New Jersey, 1965. A collection of critical essays.

TILLYARD, E. M. W.: *Shakespeare's Early Comedies*, Chatto & Windus, London, 1965.

WILSON, JOHN DOVER: *Shakespeare's Happy Comedies*, Faber & Faber, London, 1962.

Criticism: histories

ARMSTRONG, W. A. (ED.): *Shakespeare's Histories*, Penguin Books, Harmondsworth, 1972. An anthology of critical essays.

KNIGHTS, L. C.: *Shakespeare: The Histories*, Longman, London, 1962.

REESE, M. M.: *The Cease of Majesty: A Study of Shakespeare's History Plays*, Edward Arnold, London, 1961.

TILLYARD, E. M. W.: *Shakespeare's History Plays*, Chatto & Windus, London, 1944. A classic book, showing how Shakespeare was influenced by the ideas of his time. Later critics have tended to react against work such as that written by Tillyard, seeing it as imposing artificial limits on Shakespeare and taking attention away from the actual words on the page.

TRAVERSI, D. A.: *Shakespeare: From* Richard II *to* Henry V, Hollis & Carter, London, 1958.

WAITH, E. M. (ED.): *Shakespeare: The Histories*, Twentieth Century Views Series, Prentice-Hall, Englewood Cliffs, New Jersey, 1965.

WILSON, JOHN DOVER: *The Fortunes of Falstaff*, Cambridge University Press, Cambridge, 1943. A strong body of criticism found Prince Hal to be unattractive, calculating, and ruthless, either by accident or design on Shakespeare's part. This essential book shows how the character of Falstaff is deliberately blackened as the plays proceed, thus making his eventual rejection at the hands of Hal more acceptable.

Criticism: tragedies

BRADLEY, A. C.: *Shakespearian Tragedy*. Macmillan, London, 1904. One of the first books on Shakespearian tragedy, and still one of the best. Bradley insists on treating characters in the plays as if they were real people, and has a number of other moderately infuriating habits, but he is capable of marvellous insights into the plays.

CHARLTON, H. B.: *Shakespearian Tragedy*, Cambridge University Press, Cambridge, 1948. A useful though rather heavy-handed book.

DANBY, JOHN F.: *Shakespeare's Doctrine of Nature: A Study of* King Lear, Faber & Faber, London, 1951.

HARBAGE, A. (ED.): *Shakespeare: The Tragedies*, Twentieth Century Views Series, Prentice-Hall, Englewood Cliffs, New Jersey, 1965.

LERNER, LAURENCE: *Shakespearian Tragedy*, Penguin Books, Harmondsworth, 1963. A very useful anthology, containing as it does the original article that suggested Hamlet might be the victim of an Oedipus complex.

WILSON, JOHN DOVER: *What Happens in* Hamlet, Cambridge University Press, Cambridge, 1935. A blow by blow account of the play, particularly useful for those required to do detailed work on the text.

WILSON KNIGHT, G.: *The Wheel of Fire*, Methuen, London, 1949. Subjective, imaginative, and occasionally difficult interpretations of the tragedies.

Criticism: problem, romance, and late plays

LAWRENCE, W. W.: *Shakespeare's Problem Comedies*, Ungar, New York, 1931.

TILLYARD, E. M. W.: *Shakespeare's Last Plays*, Chatto & Windus, London, 1938.

TILLYARD, E. M. W.: *Shakespeare's Problem Plays*, Chatto & Windus, London, 1950.

WILSON KNIGHT, G.: *The Crown of Life*, Oxford University Press, Oxford, 1947.

URE, PETER: *Shakespeare: the Problem Plays*, Writers and Their Work Series, Longman, London, 1961. A very short but very readable introduction to the problems of the problem plays.

The actor's Shakespeare: a reading list

This is an arbitrary list, but all the books are stimulating and outside the usual run of 'criticism'.

BEAUMAN, SALLY: *The Royal Shakespeare Company's Centenary Production of Henry V*, Pergamon Press, Oxford, 1976. This includes a play-text and photographs, and is a good study of a fine production.

BERRY, CICILY: *Voice and the Actor*, Harrap, London, 1973. Both an invaluable practical handbook and a fascinating introduction to working on a text.

BROOK, PETER: *The Empty Space*, MacGibbon & Kee, London, 1968. Essential for the serious actor: the great post-war theatrical genius.

HILEY, JIM: *Theatre at Work*, Routledge & Kegan Paul, 1981. Nothing to do with Shakespeare, but an excellent book on how a production grows from inception to performance. Detailed, funny and fascinating.

SPEAIGHT, ROBERT: *Shakespeare on the Stage*, Collins, London, 1973. Excellent pictures, good text.

Index

act, 123
Adam, Old, 7
Adam and Eve, 31, 63, 124
Adams, William Bridges, 133
Admiral's Men, the, 26
Agincourt, battle of, 43
All's Well That Ends Well, 34, 47–8, 54, 105, 122, 128, 138–42
allegory, 123–4
Alonso, 118
anachronism, 124
Angelo, 47, 105–10
Angels, 30
Anger, 21
Antigonus, 110–15, 125
Antonio (*The Merchant of Venice*), 121–2
Antonio (*The Tempest*), 115–18
Antony, 50–5, 100–5
Antony and Cleopatra, 34, 50, 52, 55, 91, 100–5, 119, 120, 125, 129
appearance and reality, 51
apron stage, 19, 124
Archangels, 30
Arden, Forest of, 86–90, 95, 100, 128
Arden, Mary, 8
Ariel, 118
Aristotle, 27, 43, 44
Armin, Robert, 27, 126
astrology, 31–2
As You Like It, 7, 27, 34, 38, 39, 40, 52, 86–90, 95, 100, 103, 128, 129, 131
Audrey, 86–90
Autolycus, 110–15

Banquo, 62–6
Bardolph, 137
Bassanio, 121–2
bawdy, 124
Beatrice, 95–100, 138

Beaumont, Francis, 111
Benedick, 95–100, 138
Berry, Cicily, 139
Bertram, 48, 138–42
black comedy, 62
Blackfriars Theatre, 19, 22, 111
blank verse, 124–5
Boar's Head Tavern, 135, 136
Bohemia, 113, 114
Bolingbroke, 41
Bottom, 39, 90–5
Brabantio, 68
Breughel, 134
Bronte, Emily, 119
Brooke, Peter, 134
Brutus, 23, 120–1
bull ring fever, 69
Burbage, James, 17
Burbage, Richard, 17, 27
Burleigh House, 14

Caliban, 115–18
Capulet, 119
Cassio, 46, 67, 68, 69–70
Cassius, 120
catharsis, 125
Celia, 86–90
chain of being, 30
Cheapside, 135
Cherubs, 30
Chester mystery plays, 21
chorus, 125
Claudio (*Measure for Measure*), 47, 105–10
Claudio (*Much Ado About Nothing*), 95–100
Claudius, 46, 53, 56–62
Cleopatra, 50, 100–5, 125
comedies, 37–40
comedy, 125

Comedy of Errors, The, 34, 36
Cordelia, 44, 51, 52, 54, 71–6
Coriolanus, 34
Cornwall, Duke of, 73
correspondences, 31
costumes, 24
Cymbeline, 19, 34, 49, 129, 130

Demetrius, 90–5, 103, 133
Desdemona, 52, 66–70, 124
Destiny, 22, 54–5
Diana, 138
director, 25, 133, 134, 137–41
disguise, 39–40
divine right of kings, 32, 62
Dogberry, 39, 95–100, 126, 128
Doll Tearsheet, 76–81, 124
Dominations, 30
Don John, 52, 53, 95–100
Dowden, Edward, 35
Drake, Sir Francis, 17
dramatic irony, 127
Duchess of Malfi, The, 22
Duke (*As You Like It*), 40, 86–90
Duke Frederick, 86–90
Duke (*Much Ado About Nothing*), 40
Duke (*Measure for Measure*), 105–10, 117
Dumaine brothers, 138, 139
Duncan, 43, 46, 52, 63–5, 127

early plays, 36–7
eavesdropping, 40
Edgar, 55, 71–6, 128
Edmund, 23, 31, 53, 71–6, 128
Edward VI, 15
effects, stage, 125–6
Egeus, 91, 93
elements, the four, 27, 31
Elizabeth I, 14–17, 36, 40
Elsinore, 46
Emilia, 67
Enobarbus, 100–5, 125
eponymous, 126
Essex, Earl of, 7
ether, 31
Eve, 16
Everyman, 21, 23

Fabian, 81, 84
Fall, the, 31–2
Falstaff, 22, 40, 42, 51, 53, 54, 76–81, 84, 124, 134–8
Famous Victories of Henry V, The, 136
Fate, 22, 54, 55, 62, 66
Feeble, 137
Ferdinand, 116
Feste, 27, 39, 81–6, 114, 126, 129
Fletcher, John, 111
Florizel, 110–15, 116
folio, 26–7
fool, 126
Fool, the (*King Lear*), 27, 39, 45, 71–6, 126, 128, 129
Fortinbras, 62
Fortune Theatre, 19
France, King of, 71

Galileo, 58
Galtree Forest, 137
Ganymede, 88, 90
Gertrude, 57, 62
Ghost, 7, 19, 44, 45, 57
Globe Theatre, 19, 110, 112
Gloucester, Duke of, 71
good and evil, 53
Goodbody, Buzz, 141
Goneril, 44, 51, 67, 71–6
Granville-Barker, Harley, 133, 141
Greed, 21
Greene, Robert, 10
Guildenstern, 61, 62
guilds, 21

Hal, Prince (Henry V), 42, 52, 55, 76–81, 134–8
Hamlet, 7, 8, 19, 22, 27, 34, 35, 36, 43, 47, 53, 54, 55, 56–62, 66, 101, 121, 126, 127, 128, 141
Hamlet, 11, 45, 46, 52, 54, 55, 56–62, 64, 81, 120, 124
Hathaway, Ann, 9
Hecate, 62
Helena (*All's Well That Ends Well*), 48, 54, 138–42
Helena (*A Midsummer Night's Dream*), 92

Henry IV Part 1, 34, 41, 42, 53, 76–81, 126, 127, 130, 134–8
Henry IV Part 2, 27, 34, 41, 42, 53 76–81, 124, 127, 130, 132, 134–8
Henry IV, 41, 76–81, 134–8
Henry V, 7, 34, 41, 42, 43, (76–81), 125, 127
Henry V (Prince Hal), 42, 52, 55, 76–81, 134–8
Henry VI Parts 1, 2, and 3, 34, 36, 127
Henry VIII, 34, 127
Henry VIII, 14–15
Hermia, 92
Hermione, 19, 48, 110–15
Hero, 95–100
hierarchy, 30
Hippolyta, 91, 133
history plays, 40–3, 126–7
Holinshed, 63
Horatio, 61
Hotspur, 77, 137
humours, 31
Hymen, 87, 88

Iago, 23, 45, 46, 52, 66–70, 124
Illyria, 38, 85–6, 95, 100
imagery, 127
interludes, 22
irony, 127–8
Isabella, 47, 54, 105–10
itinerant actors, 18

James I (James VI of Scotland), 14–17, 62
Jaques, 19, 39, 86–90, 106
Jonson, Ben, 7, 10
Juliet (*Measure for Measure*), 105–10
Juliet (*Romeo and Juliet*), 19, 118–19
Julius Caesar, 23, 25, 34, 101, 118, 120–1, 124, 133
Julius Caesar, 103, 120–1
Justice Shallow, 137

Katharine of France, 52
Kempe, Will, 27, 126
Kent, Duke of, 51, 71, 73

King of France (*All's Well That Ends Well*), 138
King John, 34, 127
King Lear, 22–3, 27, 31, 34, 36, 39, 43, 44, 47, 51, 53, 66, 71–6, 84, 101, 122, 127, 128, 129, 131
King Lear, 46, 51, 52, 54, 55, 67, 71–6, 92, 94, 120, 122, 128
kingship, 32, 52–3
Kingsley, Ben, 141

Lady Macbeth, 43, 52, 62–6, 123, 127, 128
Lady Macduff, 52, 64
Lafeu, 139
Le Beau, 27
Leontes, 49, 110–15
Lord Chamberlain's Men, 25
love, 40, 51–2
Love's Labour's Lost, 34, 36, 37
Lucio, 105–10, 115
Lysander, 90–5, 103

Macbeth, 19, 30, 34, 36, 43–7, 54, 62–6, 67, 94, 101, 123, 124, 126, 127, 129, 133
Macbeth, 46, 55, 62–6
Macduff, 64, 66
Machiavelli, Niccolo, 23
madness, 55, 128
malapropisms, 39, 98, 128
Malcolm, 64
Malvolio, 38, 40, 52, 53, 81–6, 106, 122, 125
Mamillius, 111
Maria, 82, 83, 84
Mariana, 107
Mark Antony, 120–1
Marlowe, Christopher, 22
Mary I, 15
Mary, Queen of Scots, 16
masque, 128
Measure for Measure, 34, 47–8, 54, 105–10, 115, 117, 122, 128
Merchant of Venice, The, 34, 40, 118, 121–2
Mercutio, 119

Merry Wives of Windsor, The, 27, 34, 35, 40, 136
Messina, 38, 95–100
Midsummer Night's Dream, A, 34, 36, 38, 39, 90–5, 97, 103, 111, 117, 133, 134
minister, 59, 60
Miranda, 115
Mistress Quickly, 136
Montague, 119
morality plays, 21–2, 42
Much Ado About Nothing, 34, 38, 39, 40, 49, 52, 53, 94, 95–100, 126, 128, 138
music, 129
mutability, 31
mystery plays, 19–21

Napier, John, 136
Nature, 32
New Testament, the, 27
Nunn, Trevor, 134–41
Nurse, 119

Oberon, 90–5, 117
Octavius Caesar, 100, 105
Oedipus, 60
Old Testament, the, 27
Oliver, 86–90
Olivia, 51, 81–6
Ophelia, 52, 55, 56, 57, 61, 62, 124, 128
order, 28–9
Orlando, 86–90, 103
Orsino, 38, 44, 51, 81–6, 119
Osric, 27
Oswald, 71
Othello, 23, 34, 36, 43–7, 49, 52, 55, 66–70, 101, 124, 126
Othello, 46, 66–70, 111, 124

Parolles, 138–42
pastoral, 128
Paulina, 110–15
Perdita, 110–15, 116, 118
Pericles, 34
Peto, 137
Phebe, 86
Pistol, 136

Plato, 27
Poel, William, 133
Poetics, 43
Polixenes, 110–15
Polonius, 56, 57, 61
Pompey, 103
Poor Tom, 73, 76, 128
Porter, 45, 124
Portia, 40, 121–2
Powers, 30
Primum Mobile, 31
Prince, The, 23
Principalities, 30
problem comedies/plays, 39, 47–8, 105, 128, 139
proscenium arch, 25
Prospero, 115–18
Providence, 72
Puck, 92, 93
puritan, 85
Pyramus and Thisby, 91, 93, 94, 95

quarto, 26
Quince, 95

Raleigh, Sir Walter, 17
Rape of Lucrece, The, 26
Regan, 44, 51, 67, 71–6
Renaissance, 27, 31, 58–9
revenge, 59
Revenger's Tragedy, The, 22
rhetorical irony, 127
rhyme, 128–9
Richard II, 19, 34, 41, 42, (76–81), 127
Richard II, (76–81)
Richard III, 23, 34, 36, 127
Richard III, 23, 36
Rivals, The, 128
Rizzio, 16
Roderigo, 70
romance plays, 48–9, 129
Romeo and Juliet, 19, 34, 52, 91, 118–19, 120, 121, 124
Romeo, 118–19
Rosalind, 40, 52, 54, 86–90
Rosencrantz, 61, 62
Rowe, Nicholas, 123

scene changes, 129
scourge, 59, 60
Sebastian, 52, 83
second tetralogy, the, 41
self knowledge, 39, 51
Seneca, 22–3
Seraphs, 30
Shadow, 27
Shakespeare, John, 8–9
shares, 26
Shaw, G.B., 140
Sheridan, Richard Brinsley, 128
Shylock, 40, 118, 121–2
Silvius, 86
Sir Andrew Aguecheek, 27, 82, 84–5
Sir Toby Belch, 82, 84–5, 129
Sir Topas, 84
Slender, 27
soliloquy, 129
songs, 129
sonnets, 49
spheres, 27
stage directions, 129–30, 135
stoicism, 22, 54
symbol, 130

Tate, Nahum, 71
Taming of the Shrew, The, 34, 36
Tempest, The, 19, 34, 48–9, 115–18
Theatre, The, 17
Thebes, 38
themes, 50–5
Theseus, 90–5
Thrones, 30
thrust stage, 124
Time (*The Winter's Tale*), 7, 54, 113
Timon of Athens, 34

Titania, 90–5
Titus Andronicus, 22, 34, 36
Tolstoy, 134
Touchstone, 39, 86–90
Tourneur, Cyril, 22
tragedies, the, 43–7
tragicomedy, 130
Troilus and Cressida, 28–9, 34, 47–8,
    105, 128
Twelfth Night, 24, 27, 34, 38, 39, 40,
    44, 51, 52, 54, 81–6, 90, 95, 96, 100,
    119, 122, 128, 129, 131
Two Gentlemen of Verona, 34, 36

Universe, the, 31

verbal irony, 127
Venus and Adonis, 26
Verges, 95–100
Vice, 21, 22, 42
Vincentio, Duke, 47
Viola, 38, 40, 44, 52, 54, 81–6, 96
Virtues, 30

Wakefield mystery cycle, 21
Wart, 137
Webster, John, 22
West Side Story, 119
White Devil, The, 22
Winter's Tale, The, 7, 19, 34, 48–9,
    54, 109, 110–15, 116, 118, 123,
    124, 125, 129, 130
Witches, the, 19, 44–5, 54, 63, 65, 67,
    129
Wuthering Heights, 119

York mystery cycle, 21

Further titles

AN INTRODUCTORY GUIDE TO ENGLISH LITERATURE
MARTIN STEPHEN

This Handbook is the response to the demand for a book which could present, in a single volume, a basic core of information which can be generally regarded as essential for students of English literature. It has been specially tailored to meet the needs of students starting a course in English literature: it introduces the basic tools of the trade – genres, themes, literary terms – and offers guidance in the approach to study, essay writing, and practical criticism and appreciation. The author also gives a brief account of the history of English literature so that the study of set books can be seen in the wider landscape of the subject as a whole.

Martin Stephen is Second Master of Sedbergh School.

STUDYING CHAUCER
ELISABETH BREWER

The study of set books is always more interesting, rewarding and successful when the student is able to 'read around' the subject. But students faced with such a task will know the difficulties confronting them as they try to tackle work outside the prescribed texts. This Handbook is designed to help students to overcome this problem by offering guidance to the whole of Chaucer's output. An introduction to Chaucer's life and times is followed by a brief description and analysis of all his works, identifying the major issues and themes. The author also discusses contemporary literary conventions, and Chaucer's use of language.

Elisabeth Brewer is Lecturer in English at Homerton College of Education, Cambridge.

A DICTIONARY OF LITERARY TERMS
MARTIN GRAY

Over one thousand literary terms are dealt with in this Handbook, with definitions, explanations and examples. Entries range from general topics (comedy, epic, metre, romanticism) to more specific terms (acrostic, enjambment, malapropism, onomatopoeia) and specialist technical language (catalexis, deconstruction, *haiku*, paeon). In other words, this single, concise volume should meet the needs of anyone searching for clarification of terms found in the study of literature.

Martin Gray is Lecturer in English at the University of Stirling.

ENGLISH POETRY
CLIVE T. PROBYN

The first aim of this Handbook is to describe and explain the technical aspects of poetry – all those daunting features in poetry's armoury from metre, form and theme to the iamb, caesura, ictus and heptameter. The second aim is to show how these features have earned their place in the making of poetry and the way in which different eras have applied fresh techniques to achieve the effect desired. Thus the effectiveness of poetic expression is shown to be closely linked to the appropriateness of the technique employed, and in this way the author hopes the reader will gain not only a better understanding of the value of poetic technique, but also a better 'feel' for poetry as a whole.

Clive T. Probyn is Professor of English at Monash University, Victoria, Australia.

York Notes: list of titles

CHINUA ACHEBE
Things Fall Apart

EDWARD ALBEE
Who's Afraid of Virginia Woolf?

MARGARET ATWOOD
The Handmaid's Tale

W. H. AUDEN
Selected Poems

JANE AUSTEN
Emma
Mansfield Park
Northanger Abbey
Persuasion
Pride and Prejudice
Sense and Sensibility

SAMUEL BECKETT
Waiting for Godot

ARNOLD BENNETT
The Card

JOHN BETJEMAN
Selected Poems

WILLIAM BLAKE
Songs of Innocence, Songs of Experience

ROBERT BOLT
A Man For All Seasons

CHARLOTTE BRONTË
Jane Eyre

EMILY BRONTË
Wuthering Heights

ROBERT BURNS
Selected Poems

BYRON
Selected Poems

GEOFFREY CHAUCER
The Franklin's Tale
The Knight's Tale
The Merchant's Tale
The Miller's Tale
The Nun's Priest's Tale
The Pardoner's Tale
Prologue to the Canterbury Tales
The Wife of Bath's Tale

SAMUEL TAYLOR COLERIDGE
Selected Poems

JOSEPH CONRAD
Heart of Darkness

DANIEL DEFOE
Moll Flanders
Robinson Crusoe

SHELAGH DELANEY
A Taste of Honey

CHARLES DICKENS
Bleak House
David Copperfield
Great Expectations
Hard Times
Oliver Twist

EMILY DICKINSON
Selected Poems

JOHN DONNE
Selected Poems

DOUGLAS DUNN
Selected Poems

GERALD DURRELL
My Family and Other Animals

GEORGE ELIOT
Middlemarch
The Mill on the Floss
Silas Marner

T. S. ELIOT
Four Quartets
Murder in the Cathedral
Selected Poems
The Waste Land

HENRY FIELDING
Joseph Andrews
Tom Jones

F. SCOTT FITZGERALD
The Great Gatsby
Tender is the Night

GUSTAVE FLAUBERT
Madame Bovary

E. M. FORSTER
Howards End
A Passage to India

JOHN FOWLES
The French Lieutenant's Woman

ELIZABETH GASKELL
North and South

WILLIAM GOLDING
Lord of the Flies

OLIVER GOLDSMITH
She Stoops to Conquer

GRAHAM GREENE
Brighton Rock
The Heart of the Matter
The Power and the Glory

THOMAS HARDY
Far from the Madding Crowd

Jude the Obscure
The Mayor of Casterbridge
The Return of the Native
Selected Poems
Tess of the D'Urbervilles

L. P. HARTLEY
The Go-Between

NATHANIEL HAWTHORNE
The Scarlet Letter

SEAMUS HEANEY
Selected Poems

ERNEST HEMINGWAY
A Farewell to Arms
The Old Man and the Sea

SUSAN HILL
I'm the King of the Castle

HOMER
The Iliad
The Odyssey

GERARD MANLEY HOPKINS
Selected Poems

TED HUGHES
Selected Poems

ALDOUS HUXLEY
Brave New World

HENRY JAMES
The Portrait of a Lady

BEN JONSON
The Alchemist
Volpone

JAMES JOYCE
Dubliners
A Portrait of the Artist as a Young Man

JOHN KEATS
Selected Poems

PHILIP LARKIN
Selected Poems

D. H. LAWRENCE
The Rainbow
Selected Short Stories
Sons and Lovers
Women in Love

HARPER LEE
To Kill a Mockingbird

LAURIE LEE
Cider with Rosie

CHRISTOPHER MARLOWE
Doctor Faustus

ARTHUR MILLER
The Crucible
Death of a Salesman
A View from the Bridge

JOHN MILTON
Paradise Lost I & II
Paradise Lost IV & IX

SEAN O'CASEY
Juno and the Paycock

GEORGE ORWELL
Animal Farm
Nineteen Eighty-four

JOHN OSBORNE
Look Back in Anger

WILFRED OWEN
Selected Poems

HAROLD PINTER
The Caretaker

SYLVIA PLATH
Selected Works

ALEXANDER POPE
Selected Poems

J. B. PRIESTLEY
An Inspector Calls

JEAN RHYS
The Wide Sargasso Sea

J. D. SALINGER
The Catcher in the Rye

WILLIAM SHAKESPEARE
Antony and Cleopatra
As You Like It
Coriolanus
Hamlet
Henry IV Part I
Henry IV Part II
Henry V
Julius Caesar
King Lear
Macbeth
Measure for Measure
The Merchant of Venice
A Midsummer Night's Dream
Much Ado About Nothing
Othello
Richard II
Richard III
Romeo and Juliet
Sonnets
The Taming of the Shrew
The Tempest
Twelfth Night
The Winter's Tale

GEORGE BERNARD SHAW
Arms and the Man
Pygmalion
Saint Joan

MARY SHELLEY
Frankenstein

PERCY BYSSHE SHELLEY
Selected Poems

RICHARD BRINSLEY SHERIDAN
The Rivals

R. C. SHERRIFF
Journey's End

MURIEL SPARK
The Prime of Miss Jean Brodie

JOHN STEINBECK
The Grapes of Wrath
Of Mice and Men
The Pearl

TOM STOPPARD
Rosencrantz and Guildenstern are Dead

JONATHAN SWIFT
Gulliver's Travels

JOHN MILLINGTON SYNGE
The Playboy of the Western World

MILDRED D. TAYLOR
Roll of Thunder, Hear My Cry

W. M. THACKERAY
Vanity Fair

MARK TWAIN
Huckleberry Finn

VIRGIL
The Aeneid

DEREK WALCOTT
Selected Poems

ALICE WALKER
The Color Purple

JOHN WEBSTER
The Duchess of Malfi

OSCAR WILDE
The Importance of Being Earnest

TENNESSEE WILLIAMS
Cat on a Hot Tin Roof
A Streetcar Named Desire

VIRGINIA WOOLF
Mrs Dalloway
To the Lighthouse

WILLIAM WORDSWORTH
Selected Poems

W. B. YEATS
Selected Poems

York Handbooks: list of titles

YORK HANDBOOKS form a companion series to York Notes and are designed to meet the wider needs of students of English and related fields. Each volume is a compact study of a given subject area, written by an authority with experience in communicating the essential ideas to students at all levels.

AN A.B.C. OF SHAKESPEARE
by P. C. BAYLEY

A DICTIONARY OF BRITISH AND IRISH AUTHORS
by ANTONY KAMM

A DICTIONARY OF LITERARY TERMS (Second Edition)
by MARTIN GRAY

ENGLISH POETRY
by CLIVE T. PROBYN

AN INTRODUCTION TO AUSTRALIAN LITERATURE
by TREVOR JAMES

AN INTRODUCTION TO LINGUISTICS
by LORETO TODD

AN INTRODUCTION TO LITERARY CRITICISM
by RICHARD DUTTON

AN INTRODUCTORY GUIDE TO ENGLISH LITERATURE
by MARTIN STEPHEN

THE METAPHYSICAL POETS
by TREVOR JAMES

STUDYING CHAUCER
by ELISABETH BREWER

STUDYING JANE AUSTEN
by IAN MILLIGAN

STUDYING SHAKESPEARE
by MARTIN STEPHEN *and* PHILIP FRANKS

WOMEN WRITERS IN ENGLISH LITERATURE
by JANE STEVENSON

The authors of this Handbook

MARTIN STEPHEN was educated at Uppingham, the University of Leeds, and the University of Sheffield. He is at present High Master of Manchester Grammar School, and was previously a housemaster and teacher of English at Haileybury College. He is the author of six titles in the York Notes series and *An Introductory Guide to English Literature* in the York Handbook series. He is currently working on a book on the poetry of the First World War. He has made several appearances on radio and television as a folk musician, and has also worked as a professional artist. He is married with three children.

PHILIP FRANKS is a professional actor. After being educated at the University of Oxford he worked in repertory theatres in Edinburgh, Oxford, and Coventry. He has appeared on television in 'To Serve Them All My Days' and 'Love Story'. In 1981 he joined the Royal Shakespeare Company and with them has played Lysander in *A Midsummer Night's Dream*, Florizel in *The Winter's Tale*, John Darling in *Peter Pan*, and Bertram in *All's Well That Ends Well*.